101 Ways

TO Open A

Speech

HOW TO HOOK YOUR AUDIENCE FROM THE START
WITH AN ENGAGING AND EFFECTIVE BEGINNING

Brad Phillips

SpeakGood Press
1050 17th Street NW, Suite 600
Washington, DC 20036

ISBN-10: 098832203X

ISBN-13: 9780988322035

Library of Congress Control Number: 2015910313
SpeakGood Press, Washington, DC

Reviews for *The Media Training Bible: 101 Things You Absolutely, Positively Need to Know Before Your Next Interview* by Brad Phillips

"In a chaotic media landscape, Brad Phillips offers a thorough and engaging guide to getting your message out authentically and effectively."

> **Richard Harris,** Former Director of Afternoon Programming, National Public Radio and Former Senior Producer, ABC News *Nightline*

"*The Media Training Bible* is a must read for learning best practices for creating, delivering, and staying on message with the media—a reference you'll want on your top shelf."

> **Wayne Bloom**, CEO, Commonwealth Financial Network

"Everyone who speaks to the media—and anyone who might—should read *The Media Training Bible* before even thinking about doing another interview. Executives and other professionals will want to keep this invaluable resource within reaching distance for many years to come."

> **Russ Mittermeier**, President, Conservation International

"If more politicians read *The Media Training Bible*, there would be many fewer embarrassing stories about them featured on Political Wire."

> **Taegan Goddard**, Founder and Publisher, Political Wire

"The advice in *The Media Training Bible* is both timely and timeless, filled with hands-on guidance that can be applied immediately."

> **Michael Sebastian**, Former Managing Editor, PR Daily

Table of Contents

Introduction

Hi. My name is Brad Phillips, and I'm really excited to be writing this book. I've been a full-time presentation trainer for more than a decade, and I've worked with thousands of public speakers in an effort to help them improve the effectiveness of their talks. In this book, you'll learn more about how to create an interesting open and find 101 examples of good speech openers. In addition…

Wait a minute. I think I owe you an apology. That opening paragraph probably didn't grab your attention, which is an inauspicious start for a book purporting to teach you about hooking your audience from your very first words.

And yet, that type of opening is quite familiar, used by roughly 95 percent of the speakers we work with and observe in public speaking settings. It's not *bad*, per se, since it communicates real information, but it fails to take full advantage of the critical opening moments of your presentations.

Openings offer you the opportunity to influence others, establish rapport, and exhibit creativity. They allow your main takeaway points to leap *from* your mouth and *into* the minds of the people sitting in your audience.

So if you'll indulge me, I'd like to start over.

Introduction, Take Two

Can your audience form an accurate impression of you in just two seconds?

The late Nalini Ambady, a professor of psychology at Boston's Tufts University, was fascinated by that question. To answer it, she and a colleague designed a study to test whether such "thin slices" of an impression could truly be accurate.

She filmed 13 instructors as they taught their classes throughout the semester and, at the end of the term, collected student evaluations of those instructors.

Later, she edited two-second clips of those instructors and showed them—without volume—to students who weren't enrolled in those classes. Those students were asked to evaluate the instructors using several criteria, including overall competence.

Her findings were remarkable. Students who watched *only a two-second video clip* of the teachers in action formed a similar impression of the instructors as did the students who were enrolled in their classes for the full semester. (Ambady's work made its own impression, earning a starring role in Malcolm Gladwell's business bestseller *Blink: The Power of Thinking Without Thinking*.)

Other studies have found similar results. Some show that first impressions are formed within seconds, while others find they take just a few minutes to solidify. Whichever studies you choose to believe, the end results all tell a similar story: people will form opinions about you quickly and, once they do, those opinions can prove difficult to reverse.

That's not to say that your first two seconds must be unusually brilliant or that you can't reverse an uncertain first impression. We've all had the experience of changing our minds about someone else—a speaker, a staffer, even a romantic partner—after a lackluster first impression.

But it does suggest that the opening moments of a presentation are particularly important. John Medina, a developmental molecular biologist and the author of *Brain Rules*, refers to those opening seconds as "cognitive hallowed ground" and writes, "If you are trying to get information across to someone, your ability to create a compelling introduction may be the most important single factor in the later success of your mission."

The reason for that can be attributed, in part, to the "primacy effect," which posits that when given a long list of words to remember, people tend to remember the words they heard at the beginning more than the words they heard in the middle.

Many researchers believe that the primacy effect can be explained rather simply: there's less information at the beginning of a list (first one word, then a second, then a third), so it's easier to move the words you heard earliest—the ones that weren't competing against a long list of *other* words—to long-term memory. But once you get deeper into a list, it's more difficult to keep track of all of the words. The 12th word you hear has to be added to the first 11, which makes recalling it more challenging. Of course, you already know that if you've ever struggled to remember a 10-digit phone number after hearing it only once.

The presentations you deliver won't consist of reading long lists of words to your audiences, so the primacy effect may not hold perfectly in every case. A dramatic or emotional story shared in the middle of your talk may become more memorable than anything you said during your open. But the primacy effect *does* offer useful guidance about the way our brains work and retain, or "chunk," information—and it's reasonable to conclude that it applies, in full or in part, to many of the presentations you'll ever give.

To take full advantage of a presentation's precious opening moments, you'll need to do two things for your would-be audience members: get them in the tent, and get them to focus on your bright shiny object.

Get Them in the Tent

The expression "get them in the tent" originated back in the days when salespeople traveled from city to city, raising a bold-colored tent to attract a curious crowd to which they could market their wares.

Those salespeople knew that they couldn't make the sale until they got members of the community to show up—so their first goal, before "make the sale," was "get them in the tent."

Similarly, speakers should use their opens to get their audiences in the tent. You can't make the rhetorical sale—of an idea or an actual product—until the audience has committed its attention to you.

Therefore, start strong. Capitalize on those vital opening moments from your first word—or at least from *almost* your first word.

Abandon the types of opens you've likely seen numerous times—the ones in which the speaker begins by apologizing for being nervous, thanking key members of the audience for two minutes, or telling an off-topic story about something amusing that happened the night before.

Those starters, while not out of the ordinary, squander the opening moments. It's easy to imagine audience members in those settings mentally drifting away from the speaker's tent mere moments after the presenter has started talking.

Focus on Your Bright Shiny Object

Beginning with a strong open isn't enough. In fact, a powerful open that is not related to your key takeaway point can be destructive, since the audience may remember *it*, not the more important points that followed.

The open you choose *must* connect to the overall theme of your talk. Before you develop your presentation, ask yourself what your "bright shiny object" is—the one idea, more than any other, you want audience members to take away from their time with you. Your answer should be reflected in your open.

I call your one main idea the "bright shiny object" because, in successful presentations, it's so prominent and luminous that the audience can't help but to notice it. But in less successful presentations, envision your bright shiny object becoming duller—as if covered with a thin layer of dust—as your open becomes cluttered with too many ideas or buried beneath a poorly defined purpose.

The manner in which you communicate your bright shiny object is totally up to you—and that's the fun part. As this book will illustrate, you can often make the same point in 101 different ways. That gives you great flexibility to find an open that's right for *you*, one that reflects your personality, serves your specific goals and the speech topic, and allows you to put a fresh spin on older material that has started to feel a bit stale.

That concludes the second version of this book's introduction. I hope you found it more engaging than the first.

About This Book

I've always been fascinated by beginnings. Whenever I sit in the audience just before an event starts—a rock concert, an athletic event, a book reading—I find my heart rate accelerating with anticipation.

I'm not alone. Research presented by Donald Bligh in *What's the Use of Lectures?* confirms that when we watch a presentation, our hearts tend to beat fastest during the opening minute.

Given the outsize importance of the opening, it's surprising that this is the first and only book that focuses to this level of detail solely on the open itself (at least to my knowledge).

This book features 101 different types of speech openings. Although it focuses on opens, you'll inevitably find that many of them can also be used as closes or as supporting material throughout your talks. I wouldn't be surprised if you were able to integrate 20 of these opens (or more) into a single presentation. Your presentations would almost surely be more engaging if you did.

You can use all of the opens in this book by themselves, or you can combine several of them together to form, in effect, a "super open." In some of the examples you come across in this book, you'll discover several opens embedded into one.

Some of the opens are rather straightforward, while others are more creative. Some represent only slight variations on the same theme, but those slight differences can be deployed in different ways, to different audiences, at different times. My hope is that the differences among the types of opens, even if they occasionally seem small, will trigger unique thoughts, and therefore distinctive opens, for you.

There are many wonderful books that focus on more formal speech-writing and that offer dozens of examples from speeches given many decades or even centuries ago. There is a lot to be learned from those books—but this is not one of them. My focus here is on the types of presentations most commonly given by today's speaker, the ones that millions of people around the globe are probably delivering *right now*.

The book is divided into three unequal sections.

> The first section offers a short primer on opens and explains that the beginning of a presentation actually contains *three* opens: the "pre-open," the open, and the "post-open."

> The second section, which constitutes the majority of the text, has exactly 101 pages—one for each of the 101 different types of opens.

> The third section contains brief concluding advice about how to choose the right open for your talk.

Like writing a letter, sometimes all you need is the first line to get started. People who are stuck on what to say during their presentations often figure out *exactly* what to say the moment they land on the opening they want to use—it's as if the perfect open causes the rest of their speech to unravel before their eyes. Therefore, I hope these speech starters will help you brainstorm not only your opens, but your full presentations.

By reading this book, you've expressed your commitment to starting strong and, in so doing, educating, encouraging, and energizing your audiences more effectively.

On their behalf, thank you.

The Three Opens

"A bad beginning makes a bad ending."

Euripides, Greek playwright

THE PRE-OPEN

Presentation trainers disagree about whether you should launch immediately into your open or begin more subtly with opening pleasantries instead.

James C. Humes, a speechwriter for four American presidents, warns, "By starting with something pleasant but unoriginal, you'll sound dim and dull." Professional speechwriter Alan M. Perlman disagrees, writing, "You could plunge in with a stunning, mind-grabbing quote, story, or statistic...but it's risky. People often don't like to have their attention seized."

Both experts have a point, which is why my guidance lies somewhere in between.

I view the opening seconds of a presentation as a plane, racing down a runway, gaining enough speed for takeoff. Reaching sufficient speed is necessary for flight—but it only takes 30 seconds of a six-hour plane ride to do so. Similarly, your opening remarks should be short, lasting *just* long enough to allow your presentation to take off.

Examples of pre-opens include:

- "Good morning."

- "Thank you for that lovely introduction, Susan."

- "Thank you for your invitation to speak today. I've been thinking a lot about this group since Bob invited me three months ago, and one of the things that kept occurring to me is that... [*transition to open*]."

- "Welcome to the eighth annual gathering of the Charleston Women's Auxiliary. Many of you have been here since the beginning, and it's wonderful to see some familiar faces and more than a few friends."

- "We've heard some wonderful speeches about cutting-edge technologies this morning. Jane just painted an inspiring vision of the future, so I'd like to take a step back into the recent past to explain how we arrived at this moment."

For some presentations, you might not need any pre-opening remarks at all and can skip directly to your open. For others—particularly those in which you're introduced, another speaker precedes you, or the mood of the previous presentation was substantially different from yours—a short, transitional pre-open can help clear your flight path.

Your pre-open should rarely exceed a few lines because your goal is to get the audience's attention as quickly as possible. As soon as you've completed your brief pre-open, get them in the tent by moving immediately to your open.

It's worth noting that your audience will make judgments about you before you even begin speaking. For that reason, work to project a sense of calm confidence before you begin speaking. Immediately before beginning your talk, walk to the center of the room, plant yourself, look at the audience, make eye contact with a few people, and pause. Only then—after you've established a warm rapport with your audience—should you begin speaking.

THE OPEN

The open, combined with the pre- and post-opens, generally constitutes about 10 percent of your presentation (but can vary from much less to slightly more). Since the majority of this book focuses on the open, I won't address that here.

THE POST-OPEN

Many presentations begin in much the same way: with a listing of the agenda, by acknowledging a few key people in the audience, and by saying a few words about the session's format.

Those elements are necessary for many presentations, but they shouldn't appear at the very beginning. Opening with your agenda, for example—especially when accompanied by a sleep-inducing PowerPoint slide—fails to take advantage of the pivotal opening moments of a presentation.

What I propose in this book is a complete reordering of the standard opening. In this new format, you'll begin by getting your audiences in the tent with a compelling open related to your bright shiny object (and by adding a short pre-open, if necessary), and pushing more logistical items—such as the length of your talk and whether the audience will receive handouts—to your post-open.

There are two primary items in a post-open: an audience-focused agenda and logistical details.

Audience-Focused Agenda

For most presentations, it's helpful to give your audience a sense of how your talk will be structured and the main topics you intend to discuss. As Fletcher Dean writes in *10 Steps to Writing a Vital Speech*:

> "Listeners need structure just as travelers need road signs. Knowing where the speaker intends to take them reduces noise and allows their brain to focus on the message instead of the trip."

Although agendas should often be included, they should be short. Sometimes, one sentence with three main points is sufficient:

> "Today, I'll talk about how our organization exceeded its fundraising goals, what must be done to keep the momentum going, and the internal changes that need to occur to reach the next milestone."

That short agenda has another advantage: by not detailing every point you intend to cover with great specificity, you'll be able to drop or change material as time and audience interest require *without* the audience knowing that you adjusted your original game plan.

There's one problem with the sample agenda above, though: it's written from the perspective of the organization, not the audience. As the title of this section states, you should deliver a more *audience-focused* agenda.

People attending your talks want to know how your presentation will affect them, improve their lives, or offer greater clarity. For some speeches, the answer to the question "What's in it for me?" will be evident to your audience. But if it's not, you can get them in the tent by talking about the presentation in the context of *their* goals and interests, not yours.

Sometimes, simply switching words such as *me, I,* and *the company* to *you* makes a world of difference in how openly your message is received. Look how that simple adjustment changes the relevance of your agenda to the audience:

> "Today, I'll discuss how you exceeded your fundraising goals, what we can all do to keep the momentum going, and why your roles and responsibilities will be updated to further grow your professional skills and help us reach our next milestone."

Not only was the word *you* or *your* used four times in that agenda statement, but it answered the "What's in it for me?" question by explicitly mentioning an audience benefit: growing their professional skills.

Stating an audience benefit so explicitly may not be necessary for every presentation, but you should at least consider whether mentioning one (or several) would help you achieve your goals. That's important, because as the authors of the book *Telling Ain't Training* point out, "The more the learners perceive personal value in what they are learning, the more motivated they will become."

There's one final step to completing your audience-focused agenda: adding a final line or two that reinforces your bright shiny object.

> "More than anything, what I hope you take away from our hour together is that our success last year was fueled by your passionate drive to succeed. Now that we've met our fundraising target, we need to guard against becoming victims of complacency and must renew the very passion that got us to this point."

In summary, the format for this part of the post-open is a short audience-focused agenda followed by a statement of the bright shiny object.

Logistical Details

There are five main logistical details you might include in a post-open. Not every presentation requires all five; some may not need any at all. To help you determine when each is appropriate, I've included some guidance in this section.

1. Session Length

For some presentations, the length of your talk will be obvious to the audience. When speaking at a conference, for example, your talk may be listed on the agenda as occurring between specific times. But if the audience has no reliable method of gauging whether your talk is likely to last for 10 minutes or two hours, tell them how long the session will last. It's easy for audiences to become restless if they don't know when they'll be able to use the restroom, eat lunch, or get a brief mental break.

2. Breaks

For longer sessions, give your audience a break at least once every 60—75 minutes. Telling them that you're planning to do so not only helps to address the biological concerns mentioned above, but also gives audiences less incentive to check their emails and phones during the session (if they know they can check for messages during a fast-approaching break, they might be more willing to commit their full attention to you). If you announce breaks, it's important to keep to your promised timing; if not, audiences won't trust that you'll be on time for subsequent breaks.

3. Thank-Yous

It's often polite and sometimes necessary to thank your hosts. But there's no stated rule that audience acknowledgments *must* take place first. As you'll see in the example that ends this section, you often gain more by saving them until later in your post-open.

4. Questions

In some formats, the manner in which questions will be handled (if at all) will be obvious to the audience. If you're delivering a major keynote address to 4,000 people, odds are you're not going to take questions from anyone who happens to have one along the way. In those cases, there's no need to announce how you intend to accept questions.

But some formats may be a bit more ambiguous, and in those circumstances, it's a good idea to tell the audience your intentions.

For smaller audiences, it's generally best to take questions throughout your presentation and welcome participation (doing so allows you to clarify unclear points or correct misperceptions along the way). If you want to hold questions until the end—perhaps because you first want to complete a persuasive argument—inform them that you'll reserve a certain amount of time for their queries after you finish.

5. Handouts

If you plan to distribute handouts, tell the audience what they'll be getting (that helps prevent people from wondering whether they should be writing everything down). Unless the audience needs to see your handouts *during* your talk, distribute them at the end. Otherwise, you might find yourself looking out at a sea of faces that are far too busy reading your materials to pay attention to what you're actually saying.

EXAMPLE: THE THREE OPENS

This example imagines the CEO of a nonprofit addressing her staff after the organization exceeded its fundraising goals for the year. It incorporates all three opens: the pre-open, the open, and the post-open.

[*pre-open*] "Good morning, everyone."

[*open*] "When we met here a year ago, I announced a rather audacious fundraising goal for our organization. It was such a big number—so much higher than anyone here had anticipated—that you may remember there were a few audible gasps in the room when I revealed it. I suspect a few of you feared that I had lost my mind.

When I announced that target of $25 million, it seemed unreachable, impossible. It took some of you several days to get used to the idea. But then something extraordinary started happening: one by one, you started coming into my office with creative ideas about how we could reach that goal. I saw your passion growing with every conversation.

When the year ended, it turned out that I aimed too low. Much too low. You raised a staggering sum: $36 million.

Let that sink in for a moment. You raised $11 million *more* than the amount that seemed impossible just 52 weeks ago.

As a result, we can now assist tens of thousands of low-income families who we never thought we'd have the means to help."

[*post-open: audience-focused agenda*] "Today, I'll discuss how you exceeded your fundraising goals, what we can all do to keep the momentum going, and why your roles and responsibilities will be updated to further grow your professional skills and help us reach our next milestone."

And yes, there will be another audacious goal, because I know we can reach it."

[*post-open: timing/bright shiny object*] "More than anything, what I hope you take away from our hour together is that our success last year was fueled by your passionate drive to succeed. Now that we've met our fundraising target, we need to guard against becoming victims of complacency and must renew the very passion that got us to this point."

[*post-open: thank-yous*] "Two noteworthy examples of that passion are in this room. Kelly Hodges and Samir Korpal put in so many late nights last year that the alarm company once called me at home at 2 a.m. to ask about the unusual hours during which people were entering our building. On behalf of the full team, thank you very much, Kelly and Samir, for leading our efforts."

[*transition to body of speech*]

101 Ways To Open A Speech

"He therefore who fails to please in his salutation and address, is at once rejected, and never obtains an opportunity of showing his latest excellences or essential qualities."

Samuel Johnson, English writer

1 THE SUMMARY OPEN

The summary open is the most direct way to begin a presentation, one that immediately tells the audience which topics you intend to cover and how you intend to cover them.

Beginning a presentation with such a road map is, perhaps, the most common type of open, and for good reason—it's logical and sets clear expectations for the audience.

As behavioral psychologist Susan Weinschenck writes in *100 Things Every Presenter Needs to Know About People*, "In order not to overwhelm people, you need to provide context. An easy way to provide context is to use an advance organizer, which is a high-level summary of the information that is coming next."

A school superintendent, for example, might begin a talk to administrators and teachers by saying:

> "Reading and math test scores have gone down in our district for two consecutive years. You are all aware of the challenges we're facing—including larger class sizes and shrinking budgets—but we cannot afford to use those facts as excuses. We have developed a three-part plan to reverse this trend and help our students learn more effectively. I'll share with you how we came up with that plan, what changes we must implement to make the plan work, and why we believe those changes will lead to measurable results."

This type of open is straightforward and clear, and is therefore a solid starter for many presentations. But it isn't the best choice if your goal is to captivate the audience with a memorable or creative open, so consider reserving your summary of what's to come for the post-open, used only after you've begun with an open more likely to earn your audience's attention.

2 THE STATEMENT OF PURPOSE OPEN

This speech starter is a variant of the summary open, but the statement of purpose places a greater emphasis on what you hope to achieve by the end of your remarks.

Declaring your goal from the start also sends a clear message to your audience about *their* role in your presentation—whether you're asking them to embrace an idea, learn a new technique, or buy a product.

A field director for a political campaign might say:

> "In order to win this election, we need at least 400 volunteers going door-to-door in our state. I'm going to discuss how you can be part of this political campaign, tell you about our training program, and explain what would be asked of you as representatives of our campaign. We can't do this without you. By the time I finish talking, I hope you will be eager to volunteer and get started this week."

A person leading a workplace training seminar might say:

> "The purpose of this workshop is to teach you how to make the best hiring decisions possible. You'll learn how to recruit the right candidates, evaluate résumés and cover letters, and ask the right questions during job interviews. By the time we finish, you will understand the techniques and resources available to help you find and hire the best people for the job."

Like the summary open, the statement of purpose makes your intention for the presentation immediately clear, but doesn't do so in a particularly memorable manner. Therefore, consider saving your statement of purpose for your post-open.

3 THE SITUATION APPRAISAL OPEN

In their classic business text *The New Rational Manager*, Charles Kepner and Benjamin Tregoe define a "situation appraisal" as requiring five steps:

1. List threats and opportunities

2. Separate and clarify concerns

3. Consider seriousness of and prioritize concerns

4. Determine how to resolve those concerns

5. Determine the help needed to solve the concerns

For many topics and audiences, steps one and two (or one through three) are noncontroversial. Your intent in sharing them with your audience is not to introduce new information but to briefly summarize what the audience already believes to be true. As Nancy Duarte writes in *Resonate: Present Visual Stories That Transform Audiences*:

> "Accurately capturing the current reality and sentiments of the audience's world demonstrates that you have experience and insights on their situation and that you understand their perspective, context, and values."

Steps four and five (and sometimes three) are optional, as they can be controversial in some settings (whereas there's typically broad agreement on the fact that there's a problem, there's often dissent about how it should be addressed). If that's the case, focus your open on the first two or three steps to demonstrate your awareness of their issues, and leave the final two or three for later in your presentation, delivered only after you've presented sufficient evidence to support your conclusions.

This open can become the structure for your entire talk. After beginning with a brief summary of the first two or three steps (or all five, in cases where there is broad agreement), you can walk methodically through each during the rest of your presentation.

4 THE SELF-INTRODUCTION OPEN

In many circumstances, you won't have to introduce yourself at the very beginning of a talk. Sometimes, attendees will have already seen your biography on a registration webpage or in an agenda. At other times, someone else will introduce you before you hit the stage (in that case, it's a good idea to provide that person with a suggested pre-written introduction that shares your most salient experience, establishes your credibility, and helps create common ground with your audience).

But if you have to introduce yourself—because the audience doesn't know who you are and no one else is there to introduce you—keep these two points in mind.

First, simply listing your résumé highlights will bore an audience ("I attended UCLA, earned my master's at Georgetown, and then worked at a research lab in London for three years..."). Instead, try to weave your experiences into a narrative that places your life's work into context: the struggles you endured, a moment of unexpected discovery, or the biggest misperception people have about your occupation. Your self-introduction should create meaning for your audience, not seek to be comprehensive.

Second, since listing one's accomplishments can come across as boastful, it's helpful to introduce a degree of humility. The following open hits both these points.

> "My mother jokes that I was born with a microscope attached to my eye. Not too many people endeavor to spend their lives in a dark room, isolated from others, but I knew early on that would be my destiny. For 30 years, I've sat in a windowless room in a Princeton University basement, looking through an eyepiece, trying to understand the world's rarest cancers."

5 THE AUDIENCE BENEFIT OPEN

The "statement of purpose" open alludes to the importance of identifying the benefits your audience will receive while hearing you speak. But this point is so important—and should be present in so many of your talks—that it deserves its own page.

You can determine the right benefit by imagining the people in your audience thinking, Why should I care about this? What is in this for me? To help answer those questions, consider what your audience might need from your talk in order to be somehow improved by it. Although every audience is different, people tend to want many of the same things:

- Meaningful friendships and romantic relationships

- Gratifying family time

- Career advancement

- Free time to relax and pursue interests

- Financial security

Once you've identified the right audience benefit, you can begin by highlighting it. A psychology professor discussing depression might know that, statistically speaking, most people in her class are unlikely to be clinically depressed. In order to give her students a clear benefit, she might open with:

> "Almost 15 million American adults are living with depression. You might not be one of them, but someone you know—a parent, spouse, or friend—might be living with it right now and hiding it from you, perhaps due to shame or not wanting to burden you with his or her pain. But that can have a devastating impact on your relationship with your loved one, leaving you confused and frustrated by sudden changes in behavior. Do you know how to recognize the signs of depression? What to say if you suspect someone you care about is depressed? How to offer help? By the end of class today, you will."

6 THE COMMON GROUND OPEN

Most 21-year-olds graduating from college don't see themselves as having a lot in common with the president of the United States. President George W. Bush was aware of that dynamic when he delivered the Yale University commencement address in the spring of 2001, so he injected a moment of self-deprecating humor into the first minute of his remarks.

> "To those of you who received honors, awards, and distinctions, I say, well done. And to the C students, I say you, too, can be president of the United States."

That remark, which earned a hearty laugh from the crowd, created common ground by shrinking the gap between president and student.

Humor is one way to establish common ground, but any sincere expression of similarity—shared experience, goals, or interests—can help bind a speaker to an audience.

For example, a well-built fitness coach seeking to convince less fit professionals to buy his personal training services might demonstrate his understanding of their challenges (and appear less intimidating) by sharing a personal anecdote:

> "Eight years ago, I was attending college full-time and managing a restaurant at night. Between my studies and my job, I barely had time to sleep five hours a night. I can't even look at pictures of myself from back then—I gained 20 pounds in two years and couldn't fit into any of my old clothes. I know from personal experience that juggling all of your responsibilities—work, family, chores—doesn't leave a lot of time for exercise. So I've developed a practical and proven plan that will allow you to see real results from just two one-hour workouts a week."

7 THE THIRD-PARTY ENDORSEMENT OPEN

Another way to build common ground with your audience is to begin your presentation by mentioning a third party—a person, group, business, or news organization—that is respected by the audience *and* supportive of you or your work.

This open essentially allows you to borrow the other party's credibility. Citing a respected third party sends the same message to an audience as it would if that person or group had come on stage with you and personally reassured the crowd that you're worthy of their trust.

To take advantage of this type of speech opening, first learn more about the people, industry groups, and/or news organizations your audience respects, and mention any shared interests or work you've done with those parties.

This approach can be particularly helpful if you're struggling to find similarities with the group to which you're speaking: if you're an atheist speaking to a church group, a conservative speaking to a liberal group, or a teenager speaking to retirees.

A developer plotting to build a controversial new shopping center might address a community meeting by quoting an unexpectedly supportive third party.

> "I have a long history with *The Frederick News-Post*, and it's not a particularly good one. For more than a decade, the editorial board has disagreed with virtually every project our company has put forth. But they surprised me with their recent editorial on this project. They wrote, 'As opposed to some of their other proposals, this one is worthy of our consideration. A new shopping center would replace the abandoned shell of the old mall, create more than 100 new jobs, and give city residents a reason to visit the southern edge of town again.'"

8 THE RELEVANCE OPEN

If you find yourself speaking to an audience that questions whether your topic is relevant to their lives, you might begin with an open that dampens their skepticism and makes your subject's pertinence clear.

To demonstrate how easy it can be to draw a connection between your topic and an audience's interests—even when the two seem impossibly far apart—I've chosen an extreme example.

Let's say you're an art history expert who has been invited to speak to a university business class filled with future entrepreneurs. At first, you might struggle with how to make your topic—art history—relevant to impending "masters of the universe" who think in terms of start-ups, private equity, and corporate takeovers.

As you review your notes from speeches you've given in the past, you come across an example about an ancient Chinese sculptor who was considered an oddball by his neighbors. His art pushed community boundaries—and his fellow citizens, unaccustomed to such provocation, rejected him and forced him to live the life of an outcast.

But centuries after his death, that sculptor's work still survives, displayed prominently in museums around the world. It turns out that he wasn't an oddball but a visionary, misunderstood by his contemporaries but valued by future generations.

That theme—fighting against societal norms and bringing your vision to market despite the naysayers—can apply to anyone, including budding entrepreneurs. You could follow such an open with examples of other artists and collectors who faced similar obstacles but persevered, and end your talk with "lessons learned" from the art world that apply directly to today's cutting-edge business students.

9   THE AUDIENCE PRAISE OPEN

Everyone likes to be made to feel special, so lavishing praise onto your audience can lead them to open their hearts to you. But this type of open can be tricky, since praise can come across as an obvious and insincere attempt to ingratiate yourself to the audience.

For that reason, Winston Churchill preferred saving his praise for the middle of a speech. As James C. Humes wrote in *Speak Like Churchill, Stand Like Lincoln*:

> "Churchill once explained that praise in the beginning of a talk sounds like flattery, whereas the same praise wedged into the middle of the speech comes off as sincerity. He called this delayed appreciation parenthetical praise."

Still, this approach has its place as an opener and often works best during ceremonial occasions: speaking at a charity fundraiser, acknowledging a staff member's noteworthy accomplishment, or welcoming your child's spouse to the family during a wedding toast.

This type of beginning pairs well with others, particularly some of the story opens that relate anecdotes justifying the praise. Look for smaller moments that are emblematic of a larger truth. It's usually more interesting to hear about a single challenge the group faced on its way to success, one family that was helped by a charity organization, or a single action that speaks to a person's overall character than it is to hear a laundry list of accomplishments read out loud.

Complimenting your host and/or audience is also considered a polite and mandatory step in certain cultures, so make an effort to learn the protocol expected of you by the audience to which you're speaking.

10 THE CONVERSATION NUGGET OPEN

Before drafting a presentation, I often have a planning phone call with the person or committee organizing the event.

Occasionally, someone says something during that call that seizes my attention. They might share an arresting statistic, tell me a compelling story, or say something unexpected—maybe even poignant—that reflects a certain level of thoughtfulness.

Those phone conversations (or email exchanges or in-person meetings) often yield interesting material, some of which could make for an interesting lead.

You could even use material from a conversation you have with a fellow attendee or speaker at the event. For one speech, I reworked my open to include a mention of a humorous chat I had with a typically stoic speaker the day before my talk.

If you're not sure whether the content you'd like to use is "on the record," just ask. People are usually happy to allow me to use it, particularly if I reassure them that the goal isn't to shine the spotlight solely on *them*, but to use the material to help make the underlying message more memorable. And obviously, never, ever make the person you're referencing look bad in any way.

> "I spoke to Robert Simmons a couple of weeks ago. He said something that has stayed with me since, because in just one sentence, he said so much. He told me that he recently concluded he would have to discourage his children from entering his chosen profession. That's an extraordinary statement from a man who's spent the past 30 years of his life trying to improve it. And sadly, I suspect his sentiments are shared by many other people in this room. Today, I want to discuss the things we might do to make this field one that you'd be proud to have your children enter."

11 THE AUDIENCE SURVEY OPEN

Prior to some presentations, you might be able to send a physical or electronic survey to members of your audience.

Those questionnaires are typically used to gauge an audience's knowledge of, interest in, and feelings about your speech topic; that information allows speakers to plan their remarks accordingly. But those survey results also occasionally glean interesting findings that can make for a compelling open.

If you conduct a pre-presentation survey, look for unexpected results in either direction—those questions that got unanticipated low scores or surprisingly high ones. Instead of simply revealing the findings to your audience and letting the numbers stand on their own, close the loop by tying their meaning directly to the presentation you're about to deliver.

For example, I once opened a media training workshop by revealing that a stunning 85 percent of respondents said they didn't trust reporters. Several members of the audience let out a surprised laugh when I shared that result.

I then used that finding to make a statement that would serve as the underpinning of my entire talk. I told the audience that their mistrust—while not entirely unreasonable—was almost certainly hurting their media efforts, and that I'd spend our hour together encouraging them to change to their mind-set.

This open has another advantage: it increases audience buy-in. If you reveal that 75 percent of your audience said in the survey that they don't understand a subject you're planning to cover, the 25 percent who do will find it hard to hold it against you when you spend time discussing it. (If you hadn't revealed that data, one-fourth of your audience might have wrongly assumed that everyone else understood the material as well as they did.)

12 THE FIRST-PERSON ANECDOTE OPEN

There are few ways to begin a presentation more effectively than by sharing a compelling first-person story or experience.

Stories are powerful tools that serve as particularly efficient delivery mechanisms for the takeaway points that follow. While being lectured at can feel overbearing to an audience, stories can convey the same information while keeping people open to the underlying message. Stories should be relatively short, but long enough to include relevant detail and dialogue.

One of my favorite speech openings of all time came from Brian, a client who delivered a speech about new insurance products.

He told the story of a woman he met early in his career, a grieving widow named Pam, whose young husband, James, had recently died. James had been sick and out of work for three years, so they had no choice but to stop paying his life insurance premium. As a result, Pam wasn't going to get a penny from his life insurance policy, leaving her family at great financial risk. But after meeting with Pam and examining her paperwork, Brian discovered a loophole in her policy. A few weeks later, he delivered a $100,000 check to a surprised and very grateful Pam.

Brian then transitioned to the body of his presentation:

> "When I think about the power of what we do, having been to retirement parties, having sent those kids off to college and shown individuals how to pay for it, that's very powerful. But nothing was more powerful than delivering a check in the face of tragedy. That mind-set, for me, changed everything."

Suddenly, his talk was no longer about new insurance products. It became about something much more important: the life-altering impact those products could have on their customers.

13 THE PERSONAL OPEN

Audiences tend to warm to speakers who reveal something of themselves. That doesn't mean over-sharing, but rather embracing the opportunity to share your personal connection with the material: why you got involved with a cause, how a product improved your life, or what you learned from a failure.

In his book *Still Foolin' 'Em*, comedian Billy Crystal shares a story about Jack Rollins, a well-regarded producer who saw him perform early in his career. After one performance, the two men went out to dinner.

> "We had settled into a booth in a quiet restaurant when Jack said, 'I didn't care for what you did tonight.' I wanted to stab him with a fork. 'Why,' I spit out. 'Listen,' he said, 'the audience loved it, and you can do very well with what I saw, but I have no idea what you think about anything. You didn't leave a tip.'
>
> 'A tip?' I managed to ask.
>
> 'Yes, a little extra something you leave with the audience: you. … Don't work so safe, don't be afraid to bomb. Come back tomorrow and don't use any of this material; we know it works. Just talk. Let me know how you feel about things. What it's like to be a father, what it's like to be married…put you in your material. Leave a tip.'"

One memorable client delivered a bland practice presentation about the importance of mentoring young women. When she finished, I asked whether *she* had a mentor. As she began telling me about her mentor, tears streamed down her face; that person meant that much to her. As a result, her material stopped sounding impersonal and started sounding like it mattered deeply to her. When she discussed her mentor during her second practice talk, a few people in the audience were teary eyed too.

14   THE AUTOBIOGRAPHICAL OPEN

For the majority of presentations, the self-introduction open is sufficient to give audiences a sense of your background and establish your credibility. But sometimes, *you* are the best story and, in those cases, your personal story can serve as your open.

Beginning with the most compelling and relevant parts of your personal biography work for presentations in which *you*, as much as or even more than the topic itself, are key to the presentation. That can be true in many speaking situations, including those featuring people who accomplished something remarkable, successful people who lost everything, and ordinary people who had something extraordinary happen to them.

Some years ago, I attended a speech given by former CBS News reporter Kimberly Dozier, who had been critically injured while serving as a war correspondent in Iraq in 2006. For that talk, *she* was the topic—who she had been before falling victim to enemy fire, the harrowing days following the incident, and how she eventually made her way back to living a full life.

In 2015, Monica Lewinsky—best known as the intern whose late-1990s relationship with Bill Clinton threatened to take down his presidency—reemerged as a public figure with a TED Talk that began by placing her biography into her own perspective.

> "At the age of 22, I fell in love with my boss. And at the age of 24, I learned the devastating consequences…Not a day goes by that I'm not reminded of my mistake, and I regret that mistake deeply. In 1998, after having been swept up into an improbable romance, I was then swept up into the eye of a political, legal, and media maelstrom like we had never seen before."

After her autobiographical open, Ms. Lewinsky pivoted to the very personal theme of her talk: the high price of public humiliation.

15 THE DESCRIPTIVE OPEN

Shortly before his death, actor and comedian Taylor Negron gave a funny talk about his childhood that was featured on the wonderful storytelling podcast *The Moth*.

Rather than beginning with a traditional open ("I was born in Los Angeles to two very good-looking parents"), Negron wove a rich tapestry of the place and people from which he descended:

> "I was born in Los Angeles, in a house in a canyon that was in a nest of palm trees that casted these thin, unmoving shadows, like prison bars. It was very 'California Gothic.'
>
> *I* am very California Gothic. I am the child of those people that you used to see in the ads for cigarettes in the back of *Life* magazine, those handsome people that were always wearing terrycloth robes and penny loafers, smoking cigarettes, looking like they just heard the funniest joke of their life. The 'Marlboro Man' met the 'Virginia Slims Woman' and had me."

That open—a visual first-person anecdote—paints a vivid picture for audiences that allows them, in essence, to slip inside Negron's skin to see what *he* saw. (You can often create a similar effect through a third-person anecdote or detailed case study.)

Descriptive words are concrete—and that's important, because concrete terms tend to be more memorable than abstract ones. They provide audiences with "hooks"—and as Chip and Dan Heath wrote in *Made to Stick*, "The more hooks an idea has, the better it will cling to memory." You can test this for yourself: if Negron had said "my parents dressed nicely," would you have created a mental image as strong as the one you created when he said "terrycloth robes and penny loafers"?

16 THE "AHA!" MOMENT OPEN

People are inevitably drawn to stories about an "aha!" or "light bulb" moment, in which you suddenly land upon a profound insight or experience a moment of clarity that provides you with better direction about how to live your life or pursue a goal.

So many of the stories we hear and tell are based on an "aha!" insight: the "final straw" comment a romantic partner made that hastened a breakup, the advice from a boss that suddenly made everything seem achievable, or the suggestion from a self-help author that allowed you to break through your insecurities.

These stories are the ultimate "learn from the experiences of others" template. They provide guidance about how to act—but because the focus of the story is *you*, the advice doesn't come across as overbearing. For example, years ago I made a mistake that taught me an important lesson about how to treat others.

> "When I was a young staffer for ABC News, my boss put me in charge of the chyrons (the text viewers see on the screen) for that night's broadcast. One of the chyrons we needed was for Atlanta's Morehouse College. I looked up the spelling of the school online and, unbeknownst to me, the first link spelled it wrong. There we were, 10 minutes to air, and a look of horror passed over my boss's face when he saw my mistake: MOORHOUSE. He barked at the staff to fix it—and with only 10 minutes to go, my mistake risked the entire segment not being ready on time (it was, barely). After the show, I approached my boss, took responsibility, and apologized. He nodded and said, 'I can tell that you learned your lesson and that nothing I could say would make you feel worse than you already do. Therefore, I don't need to say anything else to you about it.' That moment of forgiveness has stayed with me for 20 years, and I've tried to remember to be as merciful when I see others err."

17 THE EMOTIONAL DETAIL OPEN

In 2003, a man named Rob Feeney attended a rock concert at the Station Nightclub in Rhode Island. During the show, the band's tour manager set off some pyrotechnics, which quickly caught fire and engulfed the club, trapping scores of people and preventing them from exiting. One hundred people died in the fire, including Feeney's fiancée and two of their friends.

In 2011, Feeney was asked to speak before the Chattanooga City Council in Tennessee, which was considering a requirement for bars and nightclubs to install fire sprinklers. The vote was going to be close, and advocates for fire sprinklers were trailing by one vote. The Council assigned him a three-minute time slot, which he referred to in his opening.

> "The irony is that in three minutes, about 96 of the 100 victims in the Station Nightclub fire had lost their life, including my fiancée and two of our friends...After about 30 seconds, smoke begins to fill the room, people start coughing and choking... Just over a minute into the fire, injuries start to happen. For me, a person on fire ran into us, knocking us in separate directions...Two minutes, people are on the floor, the ceiling is falling in on us, the heat is melting skin off our bones...I was one of [the people] still alive at the two-and-a-half minute mark. I crawled to try to find my fiancée and I found her sneakers... [but] I could do nothing but crawl...I basically lost my life that night."

That type of raw emotion can be too much for some audiences to handle—particularly if it catches them off guard—so it needs to be used cautiously and can *never* feel manipulative. But Feeney, who spoke through tears at moments, came across as thoroughly authentic. His emotion helped his message feel more necessary, more urgent. And largely as a result of his testimony, the Chattanooga City Council passed the fire sprinkler requirement.

18 THE THIRD-PERSON ANECDOTE OPEN

The last six opens were all different shades of *first-person* anecdotes, because the speakers were all involved in the plots of their own stories. If those speakers had heard those stories from someone else, they would become *third-person* anecdotes—which can be just as powerful. Many stories in newspapers, television news reports, and documentaries are told from the third-person perspective, as are countless conversations at the dinner table.

Try to become a sharp-eyed collector of interesting third-party stories. Instead of searching for an all-encompassing anecdote that tells a complete story, look for a smaller one that reflects a larger truth: a story of how one man survived a difficult moment, a former account of the corruption that brought down her firm, or a moving narrative told by a crime victim on the news.

These types of third-party anecdotes are frequently heard during the annual State of the Union address. In 2015, for example, President Barack Obama told the story of one Minnesota couple.

> "Seven years ago, Rebekah and Ben Erler of Minneapolis were newlyweds. She waited tables. He worked construction. Their first child, Jack, was on the way... 'If only we had known,' Rebekah wrote to me last spring, 'what was about to happen to the housing and construction market.' As the crisis worsened, Ben's business dried up, so he took what jobs he could find, even if they kept him on the road for long stretches of time. Rebekah took out student loans, and enrolled in community college, and retrained for a new career. They sacrificed for each other. And slowly, it paid off. They bought their first home. They had a second son, Henry. Rebekah got a better job, and then a raise. Ben's back in construction, and home for dinner every night. 'It is amazing,' Rebekah wrote, 'what you can bounce back from when you have to.'"

19 THE CASE STUDY OPEN

Case studies can be first- or third-person anecdotes, but generally include additional detail or provide a deeper level of analysis. (The term "case study" has a specific definition as applied to research and in certain fields, such as psychology and medicine. The term is used more generally here.)

When you open with a case study, it should be illustrative of your larger point or used as a direct parallel to your company's current situation.

In their book *Masters of Disaster: The Ten Commandments of Damage Control*, authors Christopher Lehane, Mark Fabiani, and Bill Guttentag included a detailed four-page case study about the safety problems that plagued Toyota and the corporate crisis that resulted. This partial excerpt provides a good example of the level of detail case studies can delve into.

> "In late August 2009—the same year the company became the world's number one auto brand—an off-duty California policeman was driving a Toyota Lexus that accelerated in excess of one hundred miles per hour and crashed, killing the officer and his family... At the time of the fatal accident, Toyota was well aware of quality and safety questions about unintended accelerations. The trail of evidence included data from the NHTSA (the National Highway Traffic Safety Administration—the government agency empowered to ensure automotive safety) from 2004 indicating that Toyota vehicles accounted for 20 percent of all uncontrolled acceleration accidents (compared to 4 percent in 2000); the company's own 2009 analysis into these accidents, which suggested that the cause of the uncontrolled acceleration was due to floor mats obstructing gas pedals; and an early October 2009 recall of 3.8 million cars to address concerns that the floor mats could be obstructing the gas pedal."

20 THE MULTIPLE VIGNETTES OPEN

A vignette is a brief summary of a specific event. A single vignette can appear to be an anomaly—but stacking several of them together in an opening can make the whole feel greater than the sum of its parts.

For example, a speaker discussing the effects of concussions on professional football players could begin with a series of three vignettes:

> "February 2011. Former Chicago Bears, New York Giants, and Arizona Cardinals safety Dave Duerson commits suicide. According to *The New York Times*, he 'complained to family of his deteriorating mental state during his final months.'
>
> April 2012. Former Atlanta Falcons safety Ray Easterling kills himself. According to *USA Today*, he had 'suffered through bouts of depression and insomnia, symptoms researchers have linked to repeated head trauma,' for two decades.
>
> May 2012. Former San Diego Chargers, Miami Dolphins, and New England Patriots star Junior Seau shoots himself in his chest so his brain can be preserved for research. According to his autopsy report, he had been suffering from the same form of chronic brain damage as dozens of other former football players."

To test the strength of the multiple vignettes open, go back and read just the first vignette; it likely won't produce as strong of a reaction for you as reading all three back-to-back. This device can also be used to link together several *concurrent* events, such as a story of two mathematicians who were, unbeknownst to the other, working on the same problem and who discovered the previously unknown answer within hours of one another.

21 THE LIST OPEN

The list open bears a resemblance to the multiple vignettes open, but its purpose is slightly different. It places less emphasis on any single event and lists many more of them, its goal being to leave an overall impression of quantity.

Memorial services after a public tragedy often begin this way, with a reading of the names of the victims. Although television viewers may not remember any of the people's names, they *will* remember—and be moved by—the sheer number of victims.

This device has many applications in more common presentation settings. A speaker discussing how difficult it is to open a successful restaurant might begin by referring to an infamous "cursed" location for dining establishments in New York City.

> "Le Premier. Bistro Pascal. Gnolo. Moon's. John Clancy's East. Lolabelle. Napa Valley Grill. Tucci. Tucci No. 2. Peaches. Il Patrizio. Haikara Grill. Smokin' Q. Those restaurants were all located at 206 East 63rd Street. From 1977 to 2011, that address was home to 13 different restaurants. One would come in, fail; another would try, fail; and on and on it went for 34 years. That might be an extreme case, but that cycle of failure after failure is all too common for restaurateurs. Today, I'll talk about how to break that cycle. But first, it's worth mentioning that 206 East 63rd Street has finally been put out of its misery. In 2011, it became a Buddhist monastery."

A business consultant discussing the challenges of opening a retail store might begin with the "to-do list" a new owner has to accomplish. A dance instructor could list the impressive number of steps a new class will learn by the end of the semester. A politician might list the number of issues he or she will have to vote on during the new legislative session.

22 THE FABLE OPEN

A fable is a short story, usually told through animals, that contains a moral lesson at the end.

"The Tortoise and the Hare," one of Aesop's Fables, is a classic example. In that fable, the slower-moving tortoise falls behind in a race against the speedier hare. The hare, confident in its eventual victory, takes a nap. The tortoise, slower but steadier, reaches the finish line first and wins. It's easy to see how that story could parallel many real-life competitive situations.

One key advantage of using a fable open is that, like many other forms of storytelling, it's a less direct—and often less accusatory—way of making a point. In her book *The Story Factor*, Annette Simmons writes:

> "Story is indirect, when directness won't work. Other forms of influence, like reward, bargaining, bribery, rhetoric, coercion, and trickery are too tightly focused on the desired outcome. These tactics actually stimulate resistance because they don't give people enough elbow room. Story is a more dynamic tool of influence. Story gives people enough space to think for themselves. A story develops and grows in the mind of your listener."

An Internet search for "fable examples" will turn up a long list of options, including many lesser-known fables that could connect to your message. The story known as "The Two Goats," for example, tells the tale of two goats approaching a narrow bridge from opposite ends and refusing to budge for the other, resulting in their deadly falls into a deep chasm below. Such a story could be used by a speaker to emphasize the need to negotiate, perhaps during a bruising merger, an internecine regional conflict, or a heated labor dispute.

23 THE ANALOGY OPEN

Literarydevices.com tells us that an analogy is a "comparison between two things" that "forces the reader or listener to understand the connection between them."

A few pages ago, you read about a volunteer pressing for a law that would require the installation of fire sprinklers in all bars and nightclubs. His fellow volunteers, lobbying for sprinklers in all newly built homes, faced opposition from home builders, who were concerned that sprinklers would increase the cost of homes, driving away buyers and risking their profits.

The legislators to whom the volunteers spoke were sympathetic, but tended to side with the builders. In order to overcome their objections, the volunteers drew an opening parallel to something the lawmakers were already familiar with:

> "The builders say we don't need fire sprinklers because we already have smoke alarms. We've heard that argument before, when auto manufacturers told us we didn't need air bags because cars already had seat belts. We now know that air bags save lives—and they didn't stop people from buying cars."

One client opened her speech with an analogy this way:

> "One of the most important lessons to know in business is which bridges to cross and which bridges to burn. Which companies should we partner with, and which companies should we reject?"

The second sentence in her open wouldn't have had as much impact on its own. By comparing the decisions her company would have to make to a burning bridge, she placed the choices into a significantly more visual—and urgent—context.

24 THE METAPHOR OPEN

A metaphor is a comparison of one action or object to a symbolically similar but literally different second action or object. Metaphors are a type of analogy, but distinct enough to consider separately. (Similes are similar but generally contain the word *as* or *like* to compare two things; metaphors do not.)

Here are a few examples:

> My head is spinning.
>
> He's a pig.
>
> The play ended on a sour note.

To demonstrate the impact of a well-chosen metaphor, first read this speech opener that *doesn't* contain one.

> "Most cable providers make you purchase their entire bundled service, which means you have to pay for channels you'll never watch. If you never watch the Golf Channel or Animal Planet, you have to pay for them anyway. Our company is changing that. You pick the channels you want and pay only for what you watch."

Adding a metaphor at the end of that description could dramatically alter its impact.

> "You might say we're the salad bar of cable providers."

That one line stands as a more memorable representation of the same information. And those types of metaphors may also help influence your audiences. In his book *Advanced Presentations by Design*, Andrew Abela cites research that finds that "metaphors are more persuasive than literal statements," and that "the use of one consistent metaphor increases persuasion."

25 THE CONTRAST OPEN

Contrasts, which highlight the differences between two (or among several) things, offer a bounty of options for opening a presentation. Here are several types of contrasts, some of which you'll read more about as standalone lessons in this book:

- Problem vs. solution: What is the problem, and what solutions can fix it?

- Failure vs. success: What does failure look like (typically, if you don't take a set of actions) as opposed to success (if you do)?

- Obstacle vs. opportunity: What barriers are standing in your way, and how can you get around them?

- This or that: How are these ideas or products different from one another, and what do those differences mean for us, you, or our customers?

- Pro and con: What are the advantages and disadvantages of a particular concept or approach?

- Needs vs. wants: What do you *need* in order to succeed, and what is inessential but on your "wish" list?

- Possible vs. impossible: What can and cannot be accomplished?

In his terrific book *Presentation Zen: Simple Ideas on Presentation Design and Delivery*, Garr Reynolds offers a few additional contrasts: strife vs. peace, growth vs. decline, and pessimism vs. optimism. The list of contrasts could easily number in the hundreds, almost any of which could make for a compelling open.

26 THE ALLEGORY OPEN

On the surface, Simon and Garfunkel's 1967 hit "At the Zoo" sounds like a lighthearted, even silly song about animals.

> The monkeys stand for honesty
> Giraffes are insincere
> And the elephants are kindly but they're dumb
> Orangutans are skeptical of changes in their cages
> And the zookeeper is very fond of rum
> Zebras are reactionaries
> Antelopes are missionaries
> Pigeons plot in secrecy
> And hamsters turn on frequently

But read the lyrics again while considering the political climate of the era: the United States was divided by the struggle for civil and women's rights and the escalating Vietnam War.

Suddenly, it becomes clear that the animals are symbols for different races, nationalities, and genders. The song takes on a new meaning about stereotypes and generalizations and, in its own way, mocks their foolishness.

The song is an allegory, defined by Oxford Dictionaries as "a story, poem, or picture that can be interpreted to reveal a hidden meaning, typically a moral or political one."

Study.com offers another example of an allegory, one that's easy to imagine an immigrants' rights advocate or social services agency representative using to begin a presentation:

> "A story about aliens who find themselves isolated and alone in a strange new world can be an allegory for what immigrants experience in a new country."

27 THE APHORISM OPEN

An aphorism is a concise phrase or sentence that contains a general truth. (Proverbs have a similar meaning and will be used interchangeably here.)

Let's look at a few examples of familiar aphorisms:

> Don't judge a book by its cover.

> If you can't stand the heat, get out of the kitchen.

> The show must go on.

Aphorisms are familiar to audiences and pack a lot of meaning into only a few words, so their wisdom transfers easily to the material to which you apply them.

In their book *Made to Stick*, Chip and Dan Heath write:

> "Proverbs offer rules of thumb for the behavior of individuals. The Golden Rule, 'Do unto others as you would have them do unto you,' is so profound that it can influence a lifetime of behavior."

Since aphorisms are so well known, be careful that they don't oversimplify your material or come across as cliché. One way to use them effectively is to introduce a twist.

> "We've all heard that it's a bad idea to put all of your eggs into one basket. 'Diversify!' is the mantra of the day. But we've done the opposite over the past decade. We've simplified our product line, removed items from the shelf, and placed our eggs in fewer baskets. And you know what? It's working. So pick up your eggs and pile them into this big basket. *That one basket* is our key to success."

28 THE POEM OPEN

A poem expresses complex sentiments using a premium of words. Its structure, different from standard prose, can be highly memorable and deeply evocative. Dictionary.com provides a colorful definition of a poem, deeming it "an intensely imaginative interpretation of the subject."

Many people dismiss poems as potential opens for their talks; admittedly, using one would be out of place in many settings. But poems don't have to be reserved solely for the formal occasions where they're so commonly heard, such as inaugurations or graduations.

As an example, Robert Frost's "The Road Not Taken" tells the story, from an autobiographical perspective, of a man standing at the beginning of a fork in the road.

> "Two roads diverged in a yellow wood,
> And sorry I could not travel both
> And be one traveler, long I stood
> And looked down one as far as I could
> To where it bent in the undergrowth"

In the three short stanzas that follow, the man experiences a variety of emotions after selecting one of the two paths and beginning his walk: regret for choosing the wrong path, fleeting optimism that he will eventually be able to return and walk the other one, and finally, sadness after concluding that he likely missed his opportunity to ever walk that second road, which will have a negative consequence on the rest of his life.

The poem is a metaphor for life itself, and it's easy to see how it can be used as an open for any group experiencing regret over a missed opportunity, feeling the pain of an incorrect choice, or stuck in the paralysis of an "either-or" decision.

29 THE SURPRISING STATISTIC OPEN

When people hear the term *statistics*, they generally think in terms of numbers and data. But most raw numbers don't stick unless they're set within a more meaningful context.

For example, opening by simply saying "Americans watch an average of five hours of television each day" wouldn't be as captivating as this opening, which uses a broader framing:

> "Think for a moment about where you were 16 years ago. Perhaps you were in school, or in a different job, or living in a different city. Since then, friendships and relationships have started and ended. You've watched your children become adults. Maybe your name has changed from 'Mom' to 'Grandma,' or 'Son' to 'Father.'
>
> Imagine that on one morning 16 years ago, you turned your television on. And that for every minute of those past 16 years—24 hours a day, even while you slept—you've had that television playing in front of you. Over the course of a lifetime, that's how much time the average American spends watching TV. And all of that wasted time has some very real consequences."

The following 2011 National Public Radio report illustrates that such framing is not only more interesting but potentially persuasive enough to lead to meaningful behavior change:

> "What if you knew that it would take 50 minutes of jogging to burn off one soda? When researchers taped signs saying just that on the drink coolers in four inner-city [Baltimore] neighborhood stores, sales of sugary beverages to teenagers dropped by 50 percent. That tactic was more effective than a sign saying that the drinks had 250 calories each, or a sign saying that a soft drink accounts for 11 percent of recommended daily calories."

30 THE RAPID-FIRE STATISTICS OPEN

On the previous page, I wrote that statistics without context tend not to stick. So you might be surprised that there are times I recommend "drowning" your audience with a rapid-fire series of statistics that individually don't contain much context.

Facebook COO Sheryl Sandberg demonstrated why that works when she opened her TED Talk with five quick statistics:

> "The numbers tell the story quite clearly. A hundred ninety heads of states, nine are women. Of all the people in parliament in the world, 13 percent are women. In the corporate sector, women at the top, C-level jobs, board seats, tops out at 15, 16 percent. The numbers have not moved since 2002, and they're going in the wrong direction. Even in the nonprofit world, a world we sometimes think of as being led by more women, women at the top, 20 percent. We also have another problem, which is that women face harder choices between professional success and personal fulfillment. A recent study in the U.S. showed that of married senior managers, two-thirds of the married men had children and only one-third of the married women had children."

Sandberg's quick succession of statistics doesn't succeed in making any *individual* number particularly memorable—few audience members will remember the specific figures—but works for a different reason: her drumbeat of data creates an overall *impression*.

For her purposes, it wasn't important that people watching her speech remembered any particular data point. It was more important that they remembered her broader points—such as the fact that professional women are underrepresented at the executive level—and if her opening statistics communicated *that* message to her audience, they served their purpose perfectly.

31 THE RANKING OPEN

There's something about rankings that fascinates us, whether it's where a political candidate stands in the polls, which trend is being discussed the most on social media, or which movie grossed the most at the box office last weekend.

An earlier open focused on starting a talk by citing the results of a survey conducted of audience members in advance of your presentation. But you can also use *any* relevant survey or poll, of any group of people, conducted by any credible source.

For example, a career counselor presenting to college seniors might use this open:

> "What is the most important skill employers want from this year's graduating class? The National Association of Colleges and Employers conducted a survey to find out. And hiring managers came back by saying that the skill they want from you, more than any other, *isn't* creativity, or knowledge, or communication prowess. Rather, their top answer is that they want you to have the ability to work as part of a team structure. So let's talk about the best way to work as part of a team—while still maintaining your own identity."

A speaker discussing life priorities might begin with this:

> "In 2015, an Australian palliative care nurse named Bronnie Ware recorded the biggest regrets dying people expressed to her. The second biggest regret, expressed more by men, is that they worked too hard. The biggest regret, from men and women alike, is that they lived the life others expected of them, not a life that was true to themselves. That leads to an important question: how can we work less and be truer to ourselves?"

32 | THE STARTLING STATEMENT OPEN

Beginning with a startling statement can jolt audience members to attention, interrupt their complacency, and make them slightly uncomfortable (such discomfort is occasionally a necessary prerequisite to changing their mind-sets).

In her TED Talk, called "Got a Meeting? Take a Walk," author Nilofer Merchant began with a startling statement that was relevant to every person seated in her audience:

> "What you're doing right now, at this very moment, is killing you. More than cars or the Internet or even that little mobile device we keep talking about, the technology you're using the most almost every day is this [*points to her bottom*], your tush. Nowadays people are sitting 9.3 hours a day."

After another few lines, Merchant closes her open with yet another jarring and somewhat disorienting statement:

> "Sitting has become the smoking of our generation."

Researcher Pamela Meyer, whose book *Liespotting* offers readers tools to help detect deception, started her TED Talk with a statement intended to grab attention:

> "I don't want to alarm anybody in this room, but it's just come to my attention that the person to your right is a liar."

Although this approach can be powerful, consider the impact it could have on your audience (the wrong startling statement can repel people). Some persuasive presentations or talks about difficult topics might benefit from more of a buildup rather than launching with a dramatic statement. If you're unsure how this open might be perceived, test it with a few colleagues first.

33 THE DEFINITION OPEN

Read the next sentence and think about your answer before continuing. When you hear the term *beauty*, what image comes immediately into your mind?

Did you think of a grassy field on a sunny day? A piece of art? A stunning supermodel? Something entirely different?

Even the most common words and phrases can be vague—and that can be problematic for speakers who have a more specific idea about what those terms actually mean. In those cases, it might make sense to begin by defining a key term in the manner you intend to use it during your presentation.

In 2013, best-selling business author Simon Sinek delivered a keynote address at a gala dinner in Vancouver. He opened by defining the word *leadership*, an abstract term that can be interpreted in many different ways:

> "I like this idea of leadership. I like talking about it, I like learning about it, and I like meeting leaders. But what I find very interesting is to have a discussion about leadership, very often we actually don't have a very good definition of what a leader is. And so we engage in these discussions to try to figure out sort of what leadership looks like, how we should do it. And yet, we don't necessarily have an agreed-upon definition, so let's start there. To be a leader requires one thing, and one thing only: followers. That's it. It has nothing to do with rank, it has nothing to do with position."

Sinek's definition of leadership is similar to, but more specific than, the dictionary definition of the word, which makes it an interesting way to begin. When using this open, try to avoid the somewhat cliché "The dictionary defines the term *leadership* as..." approach.

34 | THE UNEXPECTED DEFINITION OPEN

In September 1980, just two months before Americans were to choose their next president, former California governor Ronald Reagan and incumbent Jimmy Carter found themselves deadlocked at 39 percent apiece, according to a *Time* poll. The United States was mired in an economic recession at the time; inflation was in double digits and unemployment was at near-record levels.

In an effort to paint President Carter as out of touch, Mr. Reagan cleverly redefined three terms during a speech in New Jersey:

> "[Carter's] answer to all this misery, he tries to tell us that we are only in a recession, not a depression. As if definitions, words relieve our suffering...If it's a definition he wants, I'll give him one. A recession is when your neighbor loses his job. A depression is when you lose yours. And recovery is when Jimmy Carter loses his."

Rather than offer a classic dictionary definition of those terms, Reagan redefined them in an unexpected way that delighted his audience and earned enthusiastic cheers.

Redefining terms can have an oversize impact on your audience. If you're speaking to a group of "stay-at-home" parents, for example, you might redefine the term like this:

> "Unlike most people, you know *exactly* what it means to be a 'stay-at-home' parent: driving to the park so your little ones can run around, taking them to the doctor, going grocery shopping, stopping at the art supply store so they have a project on a rainy day. When you think about it, I'm not sure why we're called 'stay-at-home' parents—*we're rarely home!* It would be far more accurate to call us what we really are: 'on-the-run' parents."

35 THE ODDBALL FACT OPEN

Enter the term "strange facts" into Google, and you'll come up with millions of webpages that feature the unusual, the odd, and the downright bizarre.

To write this lesson, I did exactly that. And to show you how easy it is to work an oddball fact into your open, here are two I encountered in an article on the first link that came up, via BuzzFeed.

First, I came across a story about the Haskell Free Library and Opera House, which has the distinction of residing in two nations. According to its website, "The pride of Stanstead, Quebec, and Derby Line, Vermont…was constructed deliberately astride the boundary line separating Canada from the United States…Most of the audience sits in the U.S. to watch a show on a stage in Canada."

That fascinating fact could serve as the opening for a presentation about international cooperation or stand as a metaphor about the artificial barriers that too often separate us (among many other potential topics).

The second fact that caught my eye was about an Irish mother whose twins were delivered a world-record 87 days apart (the first was three months premature but survived; the second was born closer to full term). That story strikes me as a perfect example of perseverance and the payoff that can occur after enduring a time of nerve-racking uncertainty. It's easy to see how a speaker discussing those topics could draw a parallel.

This starter can be particularly fun to develop and allows you to deploy your creativity in wonderful ways. The biggest challenge is usually drawing a link from an oddball fact to your topic—but as you've seen in the two examples above, that may not be terribly difficult to accomplish.

36 THE NEWSCASTER TEASE OPEN

News anchors are experts at keeping viewers tuned to their programs. Before tossing to commercial breaks, newscasters often deliver a compelling "tease" intended to hook people and prevent them from flipping to a different station.

Unless you've consumed unusually little mass media, you've probably heard thousands of news teases:

> "Did the local sports team win tonight's big match against their rivals? We'll tell you, next."

> "A well-known politician got into a screaming match with reporters today. The video, after this break."

> "Which movie just earned six Academy Award nominations and leads this year's pack? Our film critic has the rundown, right after the weather forecast."

This open borrows from that technique by adding similar teases to the more traditional "summary open." For instance, you might begin a talk about the overall performance of the U.S. economy in the last quarter by saying:

> "The market sent mixed signals last quarter. Today, I'll talk about why the stock market was up, why the housing market was down, and why consumer spending hasn't budged in almost a year. Along the way, you'll learn why Ford can't seem to sell big trucks this year, why France will have more homeless retirees in five years than we have here in the United States, and why one unusual but reliable signal tells us that the same stocks that led the recent rally may soon go bust."

In that example, the second sentence contains the summary open, and the third adds the more engaging newscaster tease.

37　THE POP CULTURE OPEN

In some ways, this is the most difficult page in this book to write. Current pop culture, by its very nature, is fleeting and disposable—so any specific examples will inevitably appear dated by the time you read this.

But for the same reason it's challenging to cite a relevant example in a book intended to last for many years, it's perfect for speakers to use to demonstrate their "of the moment" cultural awareness.

Pop culture refers to anything currently in the zeitgeist: a controversial film, a hit song, an odd speech delivered by an actor at an awards ceremony, an art exhibit, a celebrity whose face seems to be plastered on every magazine cover, an unusual fashion trend, or an Internet "meme" that went viral.

In February 2015, BuzzFeed posted a photo online that drew more people to its website than ever before. The picture showed a dress and asked readers to vote for which color they thought it was. Millions of people voted. Two-thirds of voters saw the dress as white and gold. They were wrong. The remaining one-third who saw it as blue and black were right.

Anyone delivering a speech during that week in February 2015 about the dangers of certainty, incorrect assumptions, or the importance of listening to the minority could have used that hook as their lead. (To help people in the audience who might not have seen the dress, the speaker could have started by projecting a slide of it and asking people to vote before revealing the results and takeaway message.)

Pop culture can be divisive, so remember the usual admonition to avoid potentially controversial comments about gender, race, religion, sexual orientation, and politics.

38 THE BOOKEND OPEN

An open is occasionally paired with a matching close, making them both appear as unifying "bookends" for your talk. Many opens in this book can be used as the first half of a bookend.

I once worked with astrophysicist Justin Kasper, who was preparing for a talk at the prestigious Aspen Institute about sensors he and his team had developed that would become the first human-made objects to enter the solar corona. He began:

> "Let's go back 150 years, late summer of 1859, and astronomers all across the world were watching the sun because something really odd was happening. A giant dark spot larger than Jupiter was slowly emerging on the surface of the sun...What [British astronomer Richard] Carrington had seen for the first time was what goes down today still as one of the largest solar flares, or solar explosions, in recorded history...That explosion released material, flung it out into space, and just 28 hours later, speeding straight towards Earth, that material struck us, and all sorts of wild things happened...People in New York reported reading the newspaper off the glow of a red sky at two in the morning. Sparks began to fly off telegraph poles...and, for the next three days, telegraph systems around the world...shut down."

After that open, Kasper left the "Carrington Event" behind and moved on to discussing his research—but he returned to it for his close, which produced audible gasps from his audience.

> "Let's go back to that Carrington Event and ask what would happen if the Carrington Event happened today...Lloyds of London predicted $2.5 trillion worth of damage could be done just within the U.S.—and the eastern seaboard of the U.S. could be without power for up to a year."

39 THE LOCATION REFERENCE OPEN

Referring to the location at which you're speaking is one of the most time-honored presentation leadoffs.

You've almost certainly seen variations of this technique many times: a politician speaking in Pennsylvania's second-largest city beginning by praising Pittsburgh's resurgence, a musician opening a concert by thanking Dublin for such a warm reception, a scholar acknowledging the special history of Nigeria while kicking off a speech in Lagos.

This open can come across as unoriginal because, too often, speakers fail to connect their location reference to their presentation topic meaningfully ("This is my first time in Santa Barbara, and it's been wonderful walking around town. It's easy to see why you love living here!").

To make this open work, look for an authentic way to connect the place with your topic. You can mention your personal ties to the location; make a historical connection between the street, town, city, state, or country and your topic; or turn a global topic into a neighborhood one by finding a local example to bolster your argument.

A climate scientist speaking at an international conference in Anchorage, for example, could localize the opening effortlessly:

> "When this conference was scheduled for Anchorage last year, we had no way of knowing that by the time we all gathered, this city would have broken a distressing record. Last winter, for the first time in more than a century of recordkeeping, Anchorage failed to dip below zero degrees even *once*. The same was true for much of the state: many cities reported record highs. And this fits into a global pattern. According to NASA, last year was the hottest year worldwide in recorded history."

40 THE CONFERENCE THEME OPEN

In auto racing, a series of flags are used as signals to drivers. A green flag indicates the beginning of a race, a yellow advises drivers to proceed with caution, a red tells drivers the race has been stopped, and a checkered flag is used to announce the winner.

So when one Indiana-based client invited me to deliver a media training workshop at a conference that was using an Indianapolis 500 theme, I decided to incorporate the world-famous auto race into my opening remarks.

My open focused on the moments when spokespersons are on safe ground (the green), how they begin to get into trouble (the yellow), and how they occasionally meet media disaster (the red). To conclude the open, I told the audience that by the end of my talk, they would be better equipped to earn a checkered flag after their interviews—even the most challenging ones.

That opening not only integrated the theme, but also helped to organize my entire talk. I divided the body of the presentation into three equal sections—the green, the yellow, and the red—and closed with a few final tips intended to help members of the audience win the checkered flag during their next interview.

Although it's not necessary to weave a conference or event theme throughout your entire talk (a little often goes a long way), doing so can be a nice touch.

If you're not speaking at a conference, you may be able to accomplish something similar by giving your presentation a creative title. For example, if I had been speaking at an Indianapolis conference *without* a theme, I could have named my talk "Media Training: How to Earn a Checkered Flag" and explained the meaning of the title during my open.

41 THE "IN THE NEWS" OPEN

Journalists are experts in taking old stories and making them feel fresh again simply by adding catchy new openers, or leads. Those additions help make their reports feel up to date, giving audiences new reason to tune in.

No matter the topic you're speaking about, odds are that something related to it has been in the news recently. An online search for your subject will likely yield several current stories, any of which might make a good candidate for a more topical open.

For example, if your firm sells a product that helps companies secure sensitive data, search for articles about data breaches. The more recent the incident, the better (at least for your purposes).

> [*Holding up a newspaper*] "This is yesterday's *Wall Street Journal.* You may have seen this front-page story about a major data breach at an international bank. More than 400,000 customer accounts were compromised, which will cost the bank at least $4 million to remedy.

> [*Holding up three other newspapers*] These articles are about three other significant data breaches that affected three different companies *just last week.*

> That's just one week's worth of data breaches. And all four of those incidents were preventable. Had any of those businesses been using our product, they could have saved themselves millions of dollars, avoided negative press, and spared their customers unnecessary worry."

This open is a perfect option for speakers who regularly deliver the same talk to different audiences. Mentioning a current news event makes that same presentation feel fresh—to you *and* your audience.

42 THE "JUST HAPPENED" OPEN

If you find yourself at a conference or other event at which other speakers will precede you, you might have an opportunity to rewrite your open up until the moment you hit the stage.

As you listen to the other speakers, pay attention for anything you might be able to incorporate into your open. Perhaps a previous speaker mentioned a statistic that reinforces your main message or made an argument that contradicts a point you intend to make. Maybe someone in the audience asked a question that you'd like to refer back to.

Either way, being that "in the moment" demonstrates to your audience that you've been paying attention and can think quickly on your feet. But since you may not have the benefit of thinking your new open all the way through, it can be risky—and is therefore best reserved for the most experienced of speakers. Instead of completely changing the open you had planned, it's safest to briefly allude to a previous comment in a pre-open and transition to the open you had originally prepared.

A speaker at a pharmaceutical conference might say:

> "Dr. Scott mentioned a study that detailed the reasons pharmacists make errors when filling prescriptions. We agree on much of what he said, but I have a different view of one of the causes that I'll share with you today."

The speaker before me at one conference competed against a loud "drum circle" in the room next to ours. When I started my talk (by which time the drums had stopped), I said:

> "When people are defensive, they're less open to what you have to say. Therefore, we need to work to reduce their opposition and open them up to our messages. If we don't, it's as if there's a drum circle playing between us."

43 THE "THIS DAY IN HISTORY" OPEN

If you do an online search for the date of your presentation alongside a phrase such as "events in history," you'll come up with countless webpages listing events that occurred on that date. Occasionally, you'll get lucky and find something that offers a perfect link to your presentation topic.

Instead of simply citing "this day in history" factoids and moving on, use them to draw a parallel to current events, as a larger metaphor, or as the basis of a case study or anecdote.

I randomly chose the date March 19 and entered it into an online search engine. Just to give you an idea of how easy it can be to use a date in history as a hook, here are a three facts I found.

- March 19, 1928: The program "Amos 'n' Andy," remembered for its caricaturish portrayal of African Americans, debuted on radio. This could be used in a presentation about race relations or stereotypes.

- March 19, 1979: C-SPAN began running live televised coverage of the U.S. House of Representatives for the first time. This could be used for a presentation about openness and transparency in government.

- March 19, 2012: Wendy's became the second-largest fast food chain in the United States, pushing Burger King down to third place. A focus on the Wendy's part of the story could be used for a speech about competition or perseverance. A focus on Burger King could be used to discuss complacency or the risks of failing to innovate.

In addition to a specific date, you can also apply this technique to weeks (National Library Week), months (Black History Month), years (the 800th anniversary of the Magna Carta), or holidays.

44 THE TIMELINE OPEN

One of the least effective slides I see during our trainings is the timeline slide. The slide is usually intended to show a chronological progression of a company's history, an industry trend, or a physical product. While using chronology as a hook can work well, the slide itself usually diminishes its impact.

Chronology is rarely about the events themselves, but rather the context they fit within. For example, Radiostratosphere.com reports that "by the end of the 1920s, one-third of U.S. households owned a radio and by 1933 that number climbed to close to 60 percent." What makes those data points more interesting, though, is that the number of homes with radios doubled within three years *during the Great Depression, when people had significantly less disposable income*. That speaks to just how essential people found radio—and the statistics themselves don't make that context fully clear.

To develop a good chronological open, identify the specific events and dates you'd like to highlight, and then create a narrative thread that binds them all together. For example, this history of radio strings six separate facts into a single story.

> "The era of broadcast journalism began with radio in 1920. The audience was small at first. But by the end of the decade, there were three national radio networks, and one-third of U.S. households owned a radio. Just three years later, by 1933, that number climbed to 60 percent—a remarkable fact considering that so many people were buying radios during the Great Depression when they had significantly less disposable income. But by then, radio was no longer a luxury item. President Franklin D. Roosevelt delivered his first 'fireside chat' that year, making radio essential for remaining informed. Consumers deemed it *so* necessary, in fact, that 90 percent of all homes had a radio by the end of the 1930s."

45 THE CHRONOLOGY CONTRAST OPEN

In *Business Storytelling for Dummies,* authors Karen Dietz and Lori L. Silverman wrote:

> "Contrast is a very powerful and often unrecognized element in creating a compelling story. It creates both tension and interest. … Contrasts are simple binary oppositions [such as] between hot and cold, young and old, light and dark."

One powerful form of contrast compares two different time periods: the past to the future, the past to the present, or the present to the future. This type of contrast can be particularly effective for talks about a new or upgraded product or process.

For example, a presentation about recent efficiencies in the publishing industry might begin:

> "For most of the history of scientific publishing, the editing process was laborious. Even a decade ago, it still involved a lot of these [*speaker holds up a Federal Express envelope*] and these [*speaker holds up a stack of papers bound by binder clips*]. 'Collaboration' meant that we constantly had to ship our latest versions around the world, give our reviewers time to read them, and wait until their comments made their way back to us. We would then cobble together those comments into yet another new document that *itself* had to be shipped back out to everyone. We lost two months on that part of the process alone. Today, that same process can take place in a week. We can upload our newest drafts to the cloud on Monday, allow anyone with an Internet connection to respond in real time, and move onto final publication by Friday. That's real progress—and today, I'll tell you how that speed is improving scientific learning while benefitting authors, institutions, and society."

46 THE EXPERT QUOTE OPEN

Beginning a presentation by quoting an expert can help bolster your argument from the very start. An "expert" can mean someone well known and famous—an inventor like Thomas Edison, a musician such as Mary J. Blige, or an internationally regarded scientist like Stephen Hawking.

It can also refer to someone few people have heard of but whose position gives them immediate credibility: the author of a well-received book on the topic, the head of internal medicine at a respected hospital, or an engineer who has toiled in anonymity but developed a deep expertise in his or her subject area.

I occasionally begin our media training workshops with an expert quote, after which I explain its relevance to the session.

> "Legendary journalist Sam Donaldson once said, 'The questions don't do the damage. Only the answers do.' We're going to prove him right today. I'm going to ask you dozens of challenging media questions, and by the end of our session, you're going to be able to answer them without causing any damage—and, even better, while *enhancing* your credibility."

As that open demonstrates, it's best to jump right into the quote rather than announcing it (so avoid "I'd like to begin by reading you a quote from…"). Keep the quotes short; they're intended to set up your talk, not steal your thunder.

One note of caution: be sure to learn something about the person who uttered the quote and the context in which they said. In 1984, for example, Ronald Reagan was regularly introduced at reelection rallies to the strains of Bruce Springsteen's "Born in the U.S.A." His staff wrongly interpreted the song as purely patriotic instead of what it really was—a scathing indictment of the Vietnam War's aftermath.

47 THE NONEXPERT QUOTE OPEN

In 2009, New York-Presbyterian Hospital began running a series of television commercials called "Amazing Things Are Happening Here." The advertisements featured real people—including patients and parents of pediatric patients—who received care at the hospital.

Advertising Age called the campaign a "game changer," writing:

> "While testimonials are hardly a new idea in hospital advertising, New York-Presbyterian's approach stands out. Shot in polished black and white, and lacking the tear-jerking background music that characterizes many 'testimonial' style hospital ads, the films are unadorned, intimate portraits of real former patients...Not only do they...not feature actors, the ads are unscripted and their subjects appear real and natural. Heather McNamara, for instance, mispronounces the name of the hospital in a way that any nine-year-old understandably might; it wasn't edited out."

You can quote a patient, a janitor, a customer, a "man on the street," a woman you once sat next to at a dinner party, your spouse's college friend, a stranger who experienced the same situation the audience finds itself in right now, or anyone else who is unknown—but has wisdom to offer—to your audience.

This open also works for another reason: "real people" often do more to sway audiences than experts. As Robert Cialdini writes in *Influence: Science and Practice*, "We like people who are like us, and we are more willing to say yes to their requests, often in an unthinking manner." Quoting a "real person" to whom the audience relates can help strengthen the audience's bond with *you*; after all, you're the person who had the wisdom to regard a person the audience deems trustworthy as deserving of mention, so you will receive the credit from the audience.

48 THE FEEDBACK QUOTE OPEN

This open is similar to the previous one, but contains a twist that serves a different purpose.

Declarative statements are debatable. If you tell your technical design team that the new edition of the software they created is weaker than previous editions, some staffers might silently (or vocally) disagree with you and think you're wrong. But quoting someone else who provided you with feedback—a happy customer, a disenchanted client who left your firm, a reporter, a fan, a skeptic—is less subject to debate. Your team might debate the merits of the feedback, but they *cannot* debate the fact that you received it and that someone has that perception.

Feedback can come from anywhere. You can quote from a tweet about your product, your company's Facebook page, a handwritten letter, an email, or a blogger's review. It can also be effective to read a short series of comments, perhaps three or four tweets that all say similar things.

As an example, if your company has been losing market share since your new product came out, you can quote a customer who recently switched to a competitor.

> "Many of you know Felicia Chen, the chief procurement officer for the Department of Commerce. I want to share with you an email she sent me last week. It reads, 'John, it pains me to tell you that we have decided not to renew our contract with you. Ultimately, my team thought that the new version had too many flaws, and we all felt our feedback from last year hadn't been implemented in the new edition as fully as we had hoped.'
>
> If we've lost Felicia, we've lost our way. We need to talk about the fixes we must make and how quickly we can make them—before other loyal customers jump ship."

49 THE UNEXPECTED SOURCE QUOTE OPEN

Great opens sometimes run counter to an audience's preconceived expectations, surprising people and giving them reason to believe the remainder of your presentation will be more interesting than they had anticipated.

One way to surprise people is to quote a source they wouldn't expect from you. This technique can work for anyone, and is particularly effective for powerful people who "humanize" themselves by quoting someone more relatable.

For example, the imposing president of a large bank might begin a commencement speech to a graduating class by quoting Kermit the Frog:

"Life's like a movie. Write your own ending."

A senior citizen addressing her state's legislature might quote a musical artist popular with the teen set. A conventionally dressed executive might quote an edgy comedian. A religious figure might quote a sexually provocative Hollywood actress.

You can quote an unexpected *person*, as in the examples above, or from a less traditional *place* or *object*. You could quote a sign you saw hanging in a store window, graffiti on a bathroom wall, a headline from a tabloid newspaper, a television commercial, something funny your mother said, an insightful question your 3-year-old daughter asked, or an angry comment overheard in a doctor's waiting area. The sources for good material are virtually limitless.

Years ago, I began a talk by noting the cognitive dissonance I had experienced the previous day when I saw a young man on the New York City subway wearing both a prominent cross necklace *and* a profane T-shirt. I then connected that story to a point about sending mixed messages.

50 THE FRIENDLY OPPONENT QUOTE OPEN

When selecting a quote, there's an easy way to introduce an unexpected twist and catch your audiences by surprise.

Instead of looking for quotes from your supporters, look for quotes from your opponents. But search for opponent quotes that appear to support *your* position.

For example, during the national health-care debate about whether Americans should be required by law to purchase medical insurance, many Democrats (who supported such a proposal) pointed to a quote from the conservative Heritage Foundation (Republicans generally opposed the requirement).

A Democratic politician might have incorporated that quote into his or her opening remarks as such:

> "I recently read a wise quote from a well-regarded policy expert. He said, 'If a young man wrecks his Porsche and has not had the foresight to obtain insurance…society feels no obligation to repair his car. But health care is different. If a man is struck down by a heart attack in the street, Americans will care for him whether or not he has insurance.' I agree wholeheartedly with that sentiment, and I suspect most of you do, too. It may surprise you to learn that that quote comes from the Heritage Foundation. [*pause*] I thank them for their support."

Many causes and businesses can use their opponents' quotes for their own benefit. For example, if a gun rights group says, "We all agree that gun safety is critically important," an organization lobbying for stricter gun-control measures can use that line. If an environmental not-for-profit organization says, "Protecting the environment doesn't have to eat into corporate profits," a local pro-business group fighting against stricter environmental regulations can lead a presentation with it.

51 THE INCORRECT QUOTE OPEN

Writing in *Presentations That Persuade and Motivate*, Beverly Ballaro recommends using quotes "if they manage to invoke irony or humor," and offers a wonderful example from an 1876 Western Union internal memo:

> "This telephone has too many shortcomings to be seriously considered as a means of communications. The device is inherently of no value to us."

Leading a presentation by quoting someone who was wrong can help you transition to many powerful points, including the risks of false assumptions, the dangers of being slow to change, and the speed of evolution.

This, from a 1995 *Newsweek* article titled "The Internet? Bah!" could be used as a perfect example to make any of those points:

> "Visionaries see a future of telecommuting workers, interactive libraries and multimedia classrooms. They speak of electronic town meetings and virtual communities. Commerce and business will shift from offices and malls to networks and modems. And the freedom of digital networks will make government more democratic. Baloney."

Writer Andrew Solomon used this device to rather stunning effect at the beginning of his TED Talk, "Love, No Matter What."

> "'Even in purely nonreligious terms, homosexuality represents a misuse of the sexual faculty. It is a pathetic little second-rate substitute for reality, a pitiable flight from life. As such, it deserves no compassion, it deserves no treatment as minority martyrdom, and it deserves not to be deemed anything but a pernicious sickness.' That's from *Time* magazine in 1966, when I was 3 years old."

52 THE BIG PICTURE OPEN

Many people begin with a rather bland description of their company, organization, or government agency when speaking to audiences unfamiliar with their work. That's problematic for two reasons: the open is unengaging, and it's all about the speaker.

For example, many people begin with something like this:

> "Good morning. For those of you who don't know me, my name is Bill Williams, and I'm the policy director for the Association for the Advancement of Arkansas Education. AAAE is a 501(c)3 nonprofit organization with 25 employees working in four statewide offices to improve elementary and secondary education here in Arkansas."

That introduction provides useful information, but it focuses solely on *what* the organization is. In the big picture open, you'll focus first on *why* your work matters, which creates a more meaningful framing than simply relying on the *what*.

> "Here in Arkansas, we rank 50th in the United States in high school graduation rates. That means our students are among the least prepared in the nation when entering the workforce and the most likely to live in poverty for the rest of their lives. The Association for the Advancement of Arkansas Education is dedicated to changing that—and to making sure that our students get the high-quality education they need to successfully compete in the global marketplace. My name is Bill Williams, and I'm the policy director for AAAE."

The second version likely grabbed your attention more than the first. That's because the second open provided more context and immediately answered the unspoken question all audience members ask themselves: "Why should I care about this?"

53 THE SMALL DETAIL OPEN

This open, as you probably guessed, is the opposite of the previous one.

In this open, you will begin by focusing on a small detail intended to intrigue the audience—but that won't make much sense on its own without the further explanation the rest of your open (or full presentation) provides.

A speaker discussing the obesity epidemic might begin by holding up an ordinary dinner plate.

> "This is a dinner plate. When you look at it, the first thing you notice might be that it is blue and white. Or perhaps you noticed its round shape. Or maybe you observed that it is made of porcelain and has an attractive striped pattern on its wide, ridged edges.
>
> I don't see any of those things. When I look at this dinner plate, I see a solution to a major national epidemic, a potential cure toward our obesity crisis. You see, this plate is only eight inches in diameter, which is smaller than most other dinner plates. And research shows that trading a larger dinner plate for a smaller one can essentially 'trick' your brain into believing that you've eaten more than you actually have. For that reason, I'd like you to try to see this plate as I do—not as a piece of porcelain, but as an object representing health and well-being that can improve life for millions of people."

The "small" detail you select for your talk can be a physical object (like a plate), a seemingly inconsequential piece of data (that you will show contains a great deal of importance), or a single word or phrase in a much longer document that reveals in some meaningful way a hidden truth.

54 THE TOUR OPEN

The "tour" open, in which you transport an audience from the room in which they're sitting to another place or time, works particularly well for scientific or location-based presentations.

It can be used by an astronomer to discuss a "visit" to the stars, a mountain climber to describe a seldom-reached peak, or a modern-day explorer who hiked his way across a desert.

Oceanographer David Gallo, whose TED Talk "Underwater Astonishments" has been viewed millions of times, started his presentation with a straightforward open that told his audience precisely how he'd use his time on stage.

> "We're going to go on a dive to the deep sea. Anyone that's had that lovely opportunity knows that for about two-and-a-half hours on the way down, it's a perfectly, positively pitch-black world."

With that, Gallo narrated a series of awe-inducing video images featuring bioluminescent sea creatures.

You can also use this open to transport your audience to another time. While introducing Matthew Weiner, the creator of the television series *Mad Men*, author and law professor Thane Rosenbaum used these lines to take his audience back to the early 1960s, when the show was set:

> "These were the days before the Pill, before drivers buckled up with seat belts, before anyone had ever heard the words sexual harassment or civil rights, before long hair was in and Brylcreem was uncool, when no one took the surgeon general's warnings seriously or gave up red meat, when wars were always regarded as noble, when going to the moon was something Jackie Gleason said, and not something astronauts could actually do."

55 THE MNEMONIC DEVICE OPEN

When I was a child, my mother taught me the colors of the rainbow. Memorizing all seven colors would have proven difficult for me, so she used a mnemonic device familiar to many, "ROY G. BIV" (which represented Red, Orange, Yellow, Green, Blue, Indigo, and Violet), to make the task simpler.

Whether for the Great Lakes (HOMES) or the musical notes on the lines of a treble staff ("Every Good Boy Does Fine"), mnemonics have long been used to help improve recall. Speakers can take advantage of the same technique to help their audiences remember their most important points more easily.

Because mnemonics are such powerful learning aids, they're frequently used for educational purposes. The acronym "FAST" is used to train ambulance staff how to recognize and respond to stroke symptoms: Face drooping, Arm weakness, Speech difficulty, and Time to call 911. In this case, the acronym itself serves as a clever reminder to treat strokes quickly.

A nurse teaching students how to treat a sprain would likely use the familiar mnemonic "RICE," which stands for Rest, Ice, Compression, and Elevation. I know from personal experience how useful such mnemonics can be; when my wife sprained her ankle, we couldn't remember each of the four elements—but we *did* remember RICE, which reminded us of them.

Mnemonics can be used to set up the structure for your entire presentation. After introducing the mnemonic in your open, each letter will represent a different segment of your talk.

Speakers can also use repeated letters as a mnemonic device, such as "The Five Cs of Credit Analysis," or an interesting sentence, such as "Kids Prefer Cheese Over Fried Green Spinach" to represent the taxonomic ranks (Kingdom, Phylum, Class, Order, Family, Genus, Species).

56 THE VISUAL MNEMONIC OPEN

Another way to create a mnemonic-like device for your material is to open with a visual representation of the points you hope the audience will remember from your talk.

Those types of visual symbols are familiar in our daily lives. You may have seen symbols such as a pyramid that shows the different tiers one must attain to achieve self-actualization, a short staircase that shows the steps one must take to earn a professional certification, or a series of circles—ranging from hollow to completely filled in—that show different financial risk tolerances.

As an example, we use the "Message Support Stool" (below) in our media trainings as a visual reminder to reinforce a message with one of three supporting elements: stories, statistics, or sound bites. Our hope is that it serves as a useful memory trigger for trainees before each of their upcoming interviews.

Like other mnemonic devices, these can be used to set up the structure for your entire presentation; after explaining the visual in your open, you can walk through each of the steps individually.

57 THE CLIFFHANGER OPEN

A cliffhanger is a dramatic plot twist typically used at the end of a piece of fiction—a book, television show, or film—to hook the audience enough to return for the follow-up episode.

A film might end with the hero dangling precariously off the side of a cliff with his survival left in doubt ("...to be continued in part two of this series, due out next summer), a soap opera could end with the leading romantic couple on the cusp of a breakup, or a book might end with a wizard fighting a new enemy who has learned how to defeat his supernatural powers.

In the cliffhanger open, you'll introduce the beginning of an intriguing story but leave the ending hanging in the air until later in your talk.

For one talk, I started this way:

> "In my decade as a media trainer, I've asked clients thousands of practice interview questions. But there's one question that no client has *ever* been able to answer satisfactorily. I'll share that question—and give you an opportunity to answer it—in a few minutes."

Here are a few other examples of cliffhanger opens:

> "He didn't know that his wife was about to leave him. But I'll begin 15 years earlier, when he and his wife first met."

> "As a war correspondent, I've seen my share of dead bodies. But I never saw one like that before. And the story of how that body came to be abandoned in the Syrian Desert has consumed the last year of my life."

> "Just moments after finishing the best meal I ever ate, I received the worst news I ever heard."

58 THE MYSTERY OPEN

While the mystery open is similar to the cliffhanger open, its intent is less to tease events than it is to pose a specific single question and answer it, piece by piece, during the course of your presentation.

Astronaut Neil Armstrong, the first human to walk on the moon, explained why mystery works so well as a narrative device: "Mystery creates wonder, and wonder is the basis of man's desire to understand."

An article on Smithsonian.com called "Top Ten Mysteries of the Universe" poses an interesting mystery about the chemical element lithium:

> "Models of the Big Bang indicate that the element lithium should be abundant throughout the universe. The mystery, in this case, is pretty straightforward: it [isn't]. Observations of ancient stars, formed from material most similar to that produced by the Big Bang, reveal amounts of lithium two to three times lower than predicted by the theoretical models. New research indicates that some of this lithium may be mixed into the center of stars, out of view of our telescopes, while theorists suggest that axions, hypothetical subatomic particles, may have absorbed protons and reduced the amount of lithium created in the period just after the Big Bang."

A lecturer could pose this mystery to students at the beginning of a presentation, consider both prevailing theories, and offer an opinion at the end of the session.

Not all mysteries have to be answered by the end of a speech. The lecturer could leave the mystery unsolved, creating new curiosity within the students that compels them to be more interested in new research on the topic as it emerges.

59 THE INFORMATION GAP OPEN

My wife and I enjoy watching "whodunit" television shows. The basic plots of almost all of those programs are virtually identical: a crime of some sort is committed, investigators track down evidence to identify the perpetrators, and those responsible are captured and punished for their actions.

Those shows capture our attention quickly because the opening minutes expose gaps in our knowledge. We know *someone* committed the crime—we just don't know *who* or *why*.

In his paper "The Psychology of Curiosity: A Review and Reinterpretation," Carnegie Mellon University professor George Loewenstein offers an explanation for why such gaps in our knowledge often compel us to learn more.

Loewenstein concludes that curiosity is higher, on balance, when "a single piece of information can throw light on the entire problem." He calls that an "insight," which stands in contrast to knowledge obtained more incrementally. He also asserts that people who already know a lot about a topic are often more interested in learning the parts of the topic they *don't* know.

> "Consider an individual who knows the capitals of only 3 of the 50 states. Such a person is likely to frame her or his knowledge as such (i.e. that she or he knows 3 state capitals). However, a person who knows the capitals of 47 states is more likely to frame her or his situation as not knowing 3 state capitals. Thus, as information about a topic increases, one's attention is more likely to be attracted to the gap in one's knowledge."

If you're speaking to a group that already knows a lot about your topic and you can offer an insight that fills a hole in their existing knowledge, you can begin by exposing that gap—which will give them ample reason to pay attention until the end.

60 THE BREAKING TRADITION OPEN

Political conventions are rather formulaic events. Speaker after speaker walks on stage to cheering crowds, talks from behind a lectern, and exits to rousing music played by the band below.

In 1996, Elizabeth Dole, a former cabinet secretary and the wife of Republican presidential nominee Bob Dole, decided to break with that tired convention. She strode to the lectern, waited for the applause to settle, and said:

> "Tradition is that speakers at the Republican National Convention remain at this very imposing podium. But tonight, I'd like to break with tradition for two reasons: one, I'm going to be speaking to friends, and secondly, I'm going to be speaking about the man I love. And it's just a lot more comfortable for me to do that down here with you."

As she spoke those lines, she descended the stairs and walked toward the audience. Dole received rave reviews for her effort: the *Chicago Tribune* called her speech "powerful," and *The New York Times* referred to it as "one of the biggest crowd-pleasers."

More important, she parted with tradition for a reason consistent with her speech's mission: she wanted to paint her husband as more relatable to voters, and her technique sought to accomplish that through her more approachable style.

There are many ways to part with tradition: opting to do without PowerPoint in settings where its use is expected, forgoing your usual "formal" written speech and speaking with a more extemporaneous style instead, or, as Ms. Dole did, abandoning the lectern and speaking without a physical barrier separating you from the audience. Just remember: if you tell the audience why you've made those choices, your reason for doing so should be tied directly to the purpose of your speech.

61 THE CONFOUND EXPECTATIONS OPEN

People unfamiliar with Randy Pausch, a well-regarded computer science professor, might have expected him to be at least a little down while delivering a lecture to colleagues and students at Carnegie Mellon University in 2007. The 46-year-old had recently been told by doctors that his pancreatic cancer was no longer treatable and that he had no more than six months of good health remaining.

Instead, Pausch confounded the audience's expectations by opening his talk with good humor, even challenging audience members to a physical competition. His unexpected beginning set an upbeat tone that almost instantly helped divert the audience's attention away from his health:

> "If I don't seem as depressed or morose as I should be, sorry to disappoint you. And I assure you I am not in denial. It's not like I'm not aware of what's going on. My family, my three kids, my wife, we just decamped. We bought a lovely house in Chesapeake, Virginia, near Norfolk, and we're doing that because that's a better place for the family to be down the road. And the other thing is I am in phenomenally good health right now. I mean it's the greatest thing of cognitive dissonance you will ever see is the fact that I am in really good shape. In fact, I am in better shape than most of you. [*Pausch gets on floor, does several push-ups*] So anybody who wants to cry or pity me can come down and do a few of those, and then you may pity me."

An uncited author writing for the collection *Presentations That Persuade and Motivate* says that surprising the audience in this way "…not only makes your speech more interesting, [but] also suggests that you're worth listening to because you have insight into the situation that no one else has."

62 THE COUNTERINTUITIVE OPEN

For this open, you'll take a stand against broadly accepted conventional wisdom that is, in your view, incorrect. Taking the audience by surprise in this manner not only grabs their attention, but often makes them more receptive to an alternate way of thinking that might not conform to their previously held beliefs.

For example, I occasionally begin our media training workshops by making it sound like I agree with the skepticism so many people hold toward the media. At the end of my initial statement, I reveal that I disagree with their perception.

> "So much of the time, people who are interviewed by the media are misquoted, taken out of context, or are otherwise misrepresented in some way by the reporter. And we know why that happens: because reporters have their own agendas and biases that twist and shape their stories.
>
> Actually, that's not right. That happens some of the time, sure, but the majority of the time, I find that it's the fault of the person who was being interviewed. They said too much, said it wrong, or didn't say enough."

Here's an example one client used to catch an audience off guard:

> "I'm sure we'd all agree that when people reach their elderly years—and suffer from ailments such as dementia—they need to be surrounded by close family and friends who can look out for their financial interests and make sure they're not taken advantage of. Well, we'd all be wrong. It turns out that one in three people who are victims of elder abuse—34 percent—are taken advantage of by their friends and family."

63 | THE MULTIPLE CHOICE OPEN

For this open, you'll give your audience a few different choices. You might present two or three arguments described from different perspectives, or offer several solutions to a problem.

Each of the options you present must be credible. You'll discuss each of them in more detail throughout your presentation, but if you make your preferred choice too obvious from the start, you will remove any sense of anticipation from your talk.

A policy analyst for an organization promoting reform of our nation's entitlement system might begin this way:

> "Roughly half of our federal tax dollars go toward Social Security and Medicare. Politicians agree that the system is unsustainable, but the debate in Washington is always what to do about it. We usually hear three basic arguments.
>
> The people supporting Option One say that we shouldn't cut anything from entitlements, which are relied upon by our most vulnerable seniors, but should cut from other programs such as defense spending instead. Of course, many politicians refuse to cut even a dime from defense spending. The people supporting Option Two say we should implement more means testing—the wealthier the person is, the less they get in benefits. But other people say that's not fair, since those standing to lose out have already put more money into the system. Those supporting Option Three say we should raise the retirement age. Opponents say that's not fair to older workers who struggle to find work.
>
> Who's right? Today, I'll discuss which of those three ideas I believe is the most likely to put Social Security and Medicare on a sustainable path."

64 THE "MY FRIEND" OPEN

In 2011, JD Schramm, a lecturer in management at Stanford's Graduate School of Business, opened his TED Talk in Palm Springs, California with a moving story about a man named John:

> "From all outward appearances, John had everything going for him. He had just signed a contract to sell his New York apartment at a six-figure profit—and he'd only owned it for five years. The school where he had graduated from with his master's had just offered him a teaching appointment, which meant not only a salary, but benefits for the first time in ages. And yet despite everything going really well for John, he was struggling, fighting addiction and a gripping depression. On the night of June 11, 2003, he climbed up to the edge of the fence on the Manhattan Bridge, and he leapt to the treacherous waters below."

John broke every rib in his body, Schramm said, but miraculously survived and was rescued by a passing ferry. Then came Shramm's punch line:

> "I know John's story very well, because I'm John."

I call this the "my friend" open, because many people use this device by talking about their "friend," only to later reveal that they are actually speaking about themselves. It can also be used to reveal a person other than yourself, such as a parent, friend, co-worker, or child.

This open can be challenging to pull off. In order for it to work, the audience shouldn't be able to anticipate the kicker before you get there. And because the technique can feel deceptive when clumsily handled, it's often best to reserve it for sincere anecdotes and moments of genuine revelation.

65 THE "SINCE I'VE STARTED SPEAKING" OPEN

My strong preference is to begin presentations by getting the audience into the tent quickly—but this open stands as a partial exception to that guiding principle.

Imagine you're lobbying for more restrictions on tobacco sales. You want to underscore just how dramatic the health consequences of smoking are, but you've found that using big numbers hasn't had the impact with your audiences you've hoped for. The most recent group to which you spoke reacted politely, but was unmoved by your opener:

> "The Centers for Disease Control estimates that tobacco use causes more than 5 million deaths per year worldwide."

For this open, begin instead with a minute or so of warm-up. You can use a shortened version of another open, perhaps a "show of hands" question or something more banal, such as thanking a few members of the audience. You're using that warm-up to soften the ground and allow your punch line to land with greater impact. When you've finished your opening minute, you can stop, turn to the audience, and say:

> "Since I started speaking just 60 seconds ago, six people have died because they used tobacco. [*Go silent for nine seconds.*] In that nine-second silence, *someone else* died. That will happen again nine seconds from now, and nine seconds from then, and nine seconds from then. During this calendar year, 5 million people—420,000 of them from this country alone—will be dead because they used tobacco products. With your help, we're going to slow that clock down. The more people we can prevent from smoking or encourage to quit, the longer the silences will become between deaths. I think we can all agree that in this case, more silence would be a beautiful thing."

66 THE CHALLENGE OPEN

President John F. Kennedy delivered a speech before a joint session of Congress in 1961, during which he made a pledge that was fulfilled just eight years later when astronaut Neil Armstrong became the first person to walk on the moon:

> "This nation should commit itself to achieving the goal, before this decade is out, of landing a man on the moon and returning him safely to the Earth."

Kennedy's challenge was more than mere rhetoric. According to the NASA History Office, "NASA's overall human spaceflight efforts were guided by Kennedy's speech; Projects Mercury (at least in its latter stages), Gemini, and Apollo were designed to execute Kennedy's goal."

Kennedy didn't open with that line—he delivered it in the middle of his speech—but in a different context, it's easy to see how such a challenge could have been used to grab his audience from word one.

This open typically articulates a specific goal, and is often buttressed with a rallying "call to action" that challenges your audience to do something specific: support legislation, raise money, increase sales, improve efficiency, cut costs, attract more customers, donate money, or volunteer their time.

A manager hoping to motivate her sales team might use the challenge open to speak about her company's rivalry with a larger competitor:

> "I'm tired of being number two. For too long, we've been Pepsi to their Coke, Wendy's to their McDonald's, Yahoo to their Google. This year, we're finally going to become number one. Who's ready to shed our 'losing is okay' attitude, overtake our rival, and declare victory?"

67 THE PEP TALK OPEN

A pep talk is a short speech intended to rally, inspire, or motivate an audience. Commonly seen in sports locker rooms, these high-energy talks also have application in other settings: a speech to managers before an important pitch, a talk to unemployed workers who are struggling to find jobs, a sermon to parishioners who are facing a variety of challenges.

Because pep talks are short and reach a rousing crescendo, they're not typically used as opens for longer speeches. But you can borrow elements from them and deliver modified versions.

Great pep talks often have two things in common. First, they acknowledge the challenge facing the audience and, possibly, their downcast mood. Second, they often contain a story about yourself, the group to which you're speaking, or another group that was once down but rose up to achieve a difficult victory.

In the film *Any Given Sunday*, Al Pacino delivers a stirring pep talk as football coach Tony D'Amato:

> "When you get old in life, things get taken from you. That's, that's part of life. But you only learn that when you start losing stuff. You find out life's this game of inches. So is football. Because in either game, life or football, the margin for error is so small...On this team, we fight for that inch. On this team, we tear ourselves and everyone else around us to pieces for that inch...that's going to make the...difference between winning and losing...Look at the guy next to you. Look into his eyes. Now I think you're going to see a guy who will go that inch with you. You're going to see a guy who will sacrifice himself for this team because he knows when it comes down to it, you're gonna do the same thing for him. That's a team, gentlemen, and either we heal now, as a team, or we will die as individuals."

68 THE POSITIVE PICTURE OPEN

This open paints a positive picture of the future, usually in an "if-then" construct ("If we do this, then our community will look like that."). Some topics—particularly those that might leave audiences feeling hopeless and overwhelmed by the scale of the problem—are good candidates for a more positive framing.

One way to paint a positive picture of the future is to look for the success stories related to your topic. In their book *Switch,* Chip and Dan Heath wrote:

> "To pursue bright spots is to ask the question 'What's working, and how can we do more of it?' Sounds simple, doesn't it? Yet, in the real world, this obvious question is almost never asked. Instead, the question we ask is more problem focused: 'What's broken, and how do we fix it?'"

A speaker discussing domestic abuse might begin with the story of a woman who survived years of brutal abuse, left her spouse, and started a successful company—and offer a hopeful plan for how other women can escape such abuse and eventually thrive.

In 2014, President Barack Obama laid out a positive vision of the future if the world acted together to confront climate change:

> "If we act now, if we can look beyond the swarm of current events and some of the economic challenges and political challenges involved, if we place the air that our children will breathe and the food that they will eat and the hopes and dreams of all posterity above our own short-term interests, we may not be too late for them...We can act to see that the century ahead is marked not by conflict, but by cooperation... and that the world we leave to our children, and our children's children, will be cleaner and healthier."

69 THE NEGATIVE PICTURE OPEN

This open does the opposite of the previous one: it seeks to convey a calamitous consequence if no action is taken regarding your topic.

Politicians are masters of this speech device. How many times have you heard candidates claiming that a vote for their opponents would lead to immediate economic ruin and international catastrophe? But painting an "if we fail to act" vision isn't the exclusive province of politicians—almost anyone can use this technique in more ordinary speaking situations.

For example, an information technology specialist speaking to her company's board of directors might present a realistic doomsday scenario while advocating for expensive new anti-hacking software. A workplace safety regulator may warn businesses of the costs of being out of compliance by describing a company hit with financial penalties, lawsuits, and bad press. A company's chief marketer could pitch a potential new client by painting a picture of their industry three years from now, in which those who fail to respond to an emerging threat will find themselves buried in a corporate graveyard.

Painting a negative vision of the future can be effective, but it can also backfire for speakers who overwhelm their audiences with a sense of hopelessness. As Andrew Abela writes in *Advanced Presentations by Design*, "Fear appeals need to be accompanied by solutions that are perceived to be credible."

Research suggests that people are generally most concerned with preserving what they already have. As Robert Cialdini writes in *Influence: The Psychology of Persuasion*, "People seem to be more motivated by the thought of losing something than by the thought of gaining something of equal value." Therefore, consider painting a negative picture that emphasizes something your audience currently has—but that could be taken away.

70 THE "NOTHING HAS CHANGED" OPEN

One of the most difficult types of presentations to deliver is one in which you're announcing a change to a policy, procedure, or position. Since people often fear and resist change, this open seeks to reassure them that the "change" is more familiar—and therefore less scary—than they might think.

As an example, I once worked with a young woman who had to present her company's social media strategy to her board of directors, which was composed primarily of older men. They regarded social media as a folly, something the younger generation used but that didn't have value for their company. Every time she presented to them, she felt they didn't understand or care about her work. I suggested a "nothing has changed" open that went something like this:

> "I know that many people regard social media as something new. I don't. I see social networks—such as Facebook and Twitter—as doing something quite old, the same things the marketing and PR shops in your own companies were doing 10, 20, in some cases 50 years ago.
>
> The goal has always been the same: reach your customers where they are. If your customers read *The New York Times*, you'd ask a reporter from that newspaper to write about your firm. If they watched a Topeka TV station, you'd run an ad in Topeka.
>
> Social media allows us to do the same thing. It reaches our customers where they are. The names have changed: instead of reaching people primarily through daily newspapers today, we're reaching them through YouTube and Instagram. But the goal is exactly the same as it's always been—reach 'em where they are—and that's why your input remains as critical as ever."

71 THE SKEPTICAL AUDIENCE OPEN

Skeptical audiences can be untrusting for several reasons. They may be ideologically opposed to your point of view, they may have been burned before, or they may just be stuck in their ways. Because there are so many causes of skepticism, there's no one-size-fits-all approach for an opening that will persuade your audiences. But there are a few best practices that may help.

First, the stronger the audience objection, the sooner you should address it. Audiences can't hear you until they know that you "get it." For that reason, acknowledge obvious truths early. There's no purpose in trying to sell an idea or product until they've lessened their resistance and opened up to you.

Second, anticipate the major objections the audience is likely to raise, and raise them first. As Nancy Duarte writes in *Resonate*, "State the opposing points before they get a chance to refute your point. An inoculation purposefully infects a person to minimize the severity of an infection."

Third, aim to frame the open around *their* concerns, not yours.

Fourth, understanding and respecting their concerns isn't the same as being defensive. Your words should seek to acknowledge their concerns genuinely, but shouldn't lapse into defensiveness.

Fifth, know your *real* audience. You might divide your audience into three groups: the people who are opposed to you and unlikely to change their minds, the people who are undecided and therefore persuadable, and the people who are already in your camp. Identify which of those audiences is most important to achieve your goals. If it's the group in the middle, you might not agonize quite as much about changing the most intransigent minds.

72 THE RHETORICAL QUESTION OPEN

Should speakers occasionally begin with a rhetorical question? (Yes. And that *was* a rhetorical question, defined by Wikipedia as "a question asked in order to make a point rather than to elicit an answer.")

You're no doubt familiar with examples, such as "Do you think I'm stupid?" and "Children grow up so quickly, don't they?"

You might be surprised that rhetorical questions are included in the "audience interaction" section of this book, but they *do* actively engage audience members, who contemplate their responses silently. For that reason, pause for a moment or two after posing a rhetorical question to allow it to sink in.

One of the most famous rhetorical questions in political history came during a 1980 presidential debate between Ronald Reagan and Jimmy Carter. Reagan, the challenger, looked into the camera, spoke directly to viewers, and said:

> "Next Tuesday is Election Day. Next Tuesday all of you will go to the polls, will stand there in the polling place and make a decision. I think when you make that decision, it might be well if you would ask yourself, 'Are you better off than you were four years ago?'"

A physician might begin a talk by posing this rhetorical question:

> "If hospitals are places for people to heal, why are fast food restaurants allowed into hospitals?"

An advocate for school reform might start with this one:

> "We know that throwing money at our local schools hasn't improved results. So why do we keep doing it?"

73 THE MULTIPLE RHETORICAL QUESTIONS OPEN

In July 2014, 298 people—two-thirds of whom were Dutch—died when their Malaysia Airlines flight was shot down over Ukraine.

Four days later, Frans Timmermans, the Dutch minister of foreign affairs, flew to New York to address the United Nations Security Council. During his opening statement, Timmermans posed several emotional rhetorical questions in a row:

> "I've been thinking how horrible must it have been, the final moments of their lives, when they knew the plane was going down. Did they lock hands with their loved ones? Did they hold their children close to their hearts? Did they look each other in the eyes one final time in a wordless goodbye?"

Timmermans' speech demonstrates that rhetorical questions often gain power in numbers. When trying to decide between one rhetorical question and several, try it both ways. Sometimes leaving one question hanging in the air is more effective; at other times, the quick sequence helps sell the message.

Using multiple rhetorical questions has another advantage: the questions you pose rhetorically during your open can serve as the structure for your entire talk. For example, a transportation expert might begin with these three questions:

> "Would high-speed rail significantly improve our nation's transportation system? Should we really spend money on trains when there are so many other pressing infrastructure needs? And in economic terms, does it actually matter if we fall further behind the rest of the developed world, which has modern rail systems?"

After being asked in the open, those three questions would be answered, in order, during the remainder of the presentation.

74 THE HYPOTHETICAL SCENARIO OPEN

Hypothetical questions force members of your audience to make a decision, helping to turn a passive audience experience into a more active one. Examples of hypothetical questions include:

> "If you had only one year left to live, what would you do?"

> "If you suddenly became a billionaire, would you continue to work?"

The key word in a hypothetical question, the one that makes the scenario become active, is *you*. Therefore, frame questions with the word *you* in it, as in "What would *you* do in this situation?"

Suppose you're an accounting expert discussing a case in which auditors didn't report the financial irregularities they had discovered from one well-paying client. You *could* open your talk in a straightforward manner and simply lay out the facts of that case. Or, you could present that scenario as a more interesting *you*-centered hypothetical question:

> "Let's say that you're an auditor for a major accounting firm. You've been looking over the books for one of your biggest clients, and you've noticed some financial irregularities that are unusual at best and criminal at worst. You bring that information to your boss, who tells you to keep quiet and get back to work.

> You know that if you go public, you'll almost certainly lose that client, and dozens of your colleagues—your friends—will lose their jobs. If you don't, you could be charged with a crime. What do you do? [*pause*] That's the question Benjamin Harris faced in 2008, when his firm…"

75 THE "IMAGINE" OPEN

In his book *Words That Work*, pollster Frank Luntz writes:

> "One word automatically triggers the process of visualization by its mere mention: imagine."

The word *imagine* holds great power because it forces people to put themselves in the center of the action. The word helps to transform the audience experience from being mostly passive (listening) to being active (thinking).

Cognitive scientist Deb Roy kicked off his TED Talk, "The Birth of a Word," with an imagine statement that helped audience members develop their own personal visual:

> "Imagine if you could record your life. Everything you said, everything you did, available in a perfect memory store at your fingertips, so you could go back and find memorable moments and relive them, or sift through traces of time and discover patterns in your own life that previously had gone undiscovered. Well, that's exactly the journey that my family began five and a half years ago."

You can accomplish the same thing without using the word *imagine*, but your statement should trigger the same visualization process. For example, you might begin a talk to a group of stressed-out working parents this way:

> "Think about your typical weekday morning routine [*pause*]. I know it may be difficult, but I'd like you to try to picture what it would look like *not* to have to survive on barely six hours of sleep each night and, instead, enjoy a leisurely and pleasurable start to your day [*pause*]. Today, I'm going to offer you three strategies for making that seemingly impossible vision come true."

76 THE QUIZ OPEN

Earlier in the book, you read about the value of exposing an information gap to your audience, which, in many situations, arouses immediate curiosity.

One great way to accomplish that is to begin your presentation with a quiz.

This is a particularly useful technique when audience members *think* they know more than they actually do. As George Loewenstein, the Carnegie Mellon professor who studies curiosity, points out:

> "Awareness of an information gap is a necessary precondition for experiencing curiosity...One way for people to gain an accurate perception of what they do not know is to have them make guesses and receive accuracy feedback. It is difficult to ignore or deny a gap in one's knowledge when one has guessed the answer to a question and been told that it is wrong."

Quizzes can also be used at the beginning and end of a workshop to demonstrate the learning that occurred during the session. Participants who got the answers wrong at the beginning should be able to answer them correctly at the end, giving them an increased sense of confidence with the material you presented.

To create an upbeat and encouraging environment from the beginning of a talk, you can also give out small door prizes to people who answer your questions correctly—perhaps a gift card to a local coffee shop, a branded mug, or one of your company's products. I occasionally give out a copy of one of my books (which is a more subtle way of letting the audience know I have a book available than overtly encouraging them to buy it).

77 THE PUZZLE OPEN

Before reading any further, cover the rest of this page with your hand so you can only read one line at a time.

For this exercise, don't think about your answer—just *quickly* count the number of times the letter *F* appears in this sentence:

> "Finished files are the result of years of scientific study combined with the experience of years."

Did you guess three? Most people do. I did too. But the real answer is six. The people at sharpbrains.com, where that puzzle appears, hypothesize that most people count three F's because "the brain cannot correctly process the word 'of.'"

These types of brain teasers, mind puzzles, and optical illusions trick our brains and capture our attention. And they can be used to make all sorts of relevant points to our audiences.

As an example, that type of open would be useful for a speaker facing an audience that is overly confident in their assumptions regarding the speech topic. Just like that puzzle, the speaker might say, what seems obvious to us is often wrong.

Another type of puzzle involves writing numbers on a board, then explaining the significance of each. For example, a speaker discussing the importance of location in real estate might write down two numbers—$168,000 and $269,000—and reveal that those homes are *identical* with only one difference: their proximity to the nearest Starbucks location. (That research was really conducted in 2015 by the CEO and an economist for Zillow, an online real estate database that contains 110 million homes.) To add even more intrigue, the speaker could write those numbers on the board before the presentation begins so audience members see them upon entering the room, but wait to reveal their meaning until the end of the open.

78 THE COMMITMENT OPEN

Let's say you're a legislator aiming to increase support for foreign aid. Your research shows that the public vastly overestimates the percentage of the budget that is spent on such purposes, and their incorrect perception fuels their opposition.

You could begin by rattling off statistics, citing data that show the difference between the *actual* percentage of the budget spent on aid versus what people *think* that percentage is.

You could also put up a slide with the following question and ask people to guess for themselves what the answer is:

> *What percentage of the United States budget is spent each year on foreign aid?**
>
> a. *1 percent*
>
> b. *15 percent*
>
> c. *28 percent*
>
> d. *36 percent*

But there's a more persuasive way to get the audience to change their minds: get them to own their answers. You can do that by asking audience members to raise their hands ("How many of you think the answer is (a)? How about (b)?"). That public commitment forces people to make their answers known to their seatmates—so when their answers are revealed to be incorrect, they can't pretend to have known the correct answer all along.

The commitment open is a wonderful technique for pointing out and correcting misconceptions. Just make sure you're likely to get the incorrect response you anticipate; if most of your audience guesses correctly, your open will lose its power.

*Answer: (a). In 2013, a Kaiser Family Foundation poll showed that the public guessed 28 percent; the actual number was 1 percent.

79 THE SHOW OF HANDS OPEN

One of the most overused presentation starters is the "show of hands" question. The problem isn't usually with the device itself, but with the ham-handed manner in which it's used.

Too often, speakers ask a question that leads nowhere: "How many of you have used this new product? Oh, okay, great." Worse, they ask a patronizing question: "How many of you would like to earn more money?" Audiences bristle at such condescensions. Participation for its own sake isn't enough.

The question you pose should challenge conventional thinking, lead to a counterintuitive conclusion, or add an unexpected dose of humor. It should allow members of the audience to see how their answers compare to those of their peers, perhaps leading them to reconsider their previously held positions.

Great opening questions must lead somewhere, so connect the audience's response to your next comment—and prepare several different transitions in case you receive an unexpected result.

For example, an expert in body image research might ask:

> "If given a choice, who here would rather be completely blind—for the rest of your life—than obese?"

Assuming very few people raise a hand, the expert could connect the audience's response to the main point this way:

> "It appears that this audience would overwhelmingly choose the gift of sight, even if that means living as an obese person. But you're not the norm. Research from Arizona State University found that one in seven women would prefer blindness to obesity. That tells you a lot about how much emphasis our culture places on physical appearance—and that comes at a high cost to our health."

80 THE SHOW OF HANDS TWO-STEP OPEN

The show of hands technique can also be used to ask *two* questions, but with sufficient time between the two to introduce new information that might change people's minds, challenge their perceptions, or expose gaps in their knowledge.

I asked one audience of business owners to raise their hands if they thought their companies were at risk of an incident that could trigger a corporate crisis. Roughly 20 percent of the people in the audience raised their hands.

Then I pulled out a copy of my first book, *The Media Training Bible*, and read from the page that lists dozens of potential crises—everything from weather-related events, product recalls, and defective products to customer complaints, controversial policy changes, and layoffs.

Then came my second question, which, in this case, was the same as the first:

> "Now that you've heard that list, how many of you think you're at risk of an incident that could lead to a corporate crisis?"

Almost every hand went up. In just two minutes, three-quarters of the attendees changed their minds, making the material that followed feel relevant to *everyone* in the room, not just 20 percent.

While this open has obvious advantages, it also has one significant drawback: if you don't get the response you anticipated from your second question, your entire opening could backfire.

Therefore, save this technique for those times when you have confidence in the audience's response—and have a backup plan in case things don't go as planned.

81 THE DIAGNOSTIC QUESTION OPEN

Many of our clients tell us that they're terrified at the beginning of their presentations but that they relax the moment they begin interacting with their audiences. That begs a question: Why not interact with the audience from the very beginning?

The key to any form of audience interaction is to engage *meaningfully*—and one great way do that is to ask "diagnostic" questions of your audience.

As opposed to a "show of hands" open, in which members of the audience typically raise their hands but don't speak, this open encourages spoken feedback.

You can direct your diagnostic question(s) to people you select at random or ask for volunteers. Ask specific, targeted questions about their concerns, challenges, goals, or hopes.

Let's say you're a professor leading a review session prior to an exam. You might begin by asking a question intended to understand the students' biggest concerns:

> "Rhonda, out of all of the material that will be covered by this exam, what are you struggling with most?"

Often, Rhonda will respond by citing a topic you had already planned to cover. If that's the case, you can refer back to her when you get to that part of your presentation, making that information feel more personal, as if you added it just for her:

> "Rhonda, you mentioned earlier that you were struggling with cell division. Let's discuss that now."

Occasionally, Rhonda may respond with something you *didn't* plan to cover. If that's the case, her reply provides you with useful information that allows you to address her concerns and make the session more relevant for her.

82 THE VOLUNTEER OPEN

Apollo Robbins, a magician best known for his stunning (and somewhat terrifying) ability to pick pockets, delivered a TED Talk in 2013 during which he selected a volunteer to come up on stage with him. The volunteer, named Joe, *knew* that Robbins was trying to take items off his person. Still, Robbins had no trouble taking Joe's watch off his wrist and removing cash from his pocket without Joe's realizing it was happening.

Strictly speaking, Joe didn't volunteer—he was asked by Robbins to join him on stage. But whether you select your "volunteer" or ask someone to join you in a more voluntary fashion, opening by having someone from the audience join you on stage can work in many public speaking settings.

For example, if you want to demonstrate how much easier your product is to use than an existing one on the market, you might ask the volunteer to first try the other product and then yours. Or you can ask the volunteer to just try your competitor's product, which you know won't be easy to use. Or to just try yours, which you're confident will work. (Scientific experiments and "how to" topics also lend themselves to this open.)

Because asking a volunteer to join you on stage introduces an uncertain variable at the very beginning of your talk, we usually recommend that this technique be reserved for more seasoned speakers.

A few more rules of thumb to keep in mind with this open: people who are selected by you without volunteering are often uncomfortable being thrust suddenly onto the stage. Make them look good, compliment them, and define their role by asking them specific questions or assigning specific tasks. Finally, their presence on stage shouldn't just be a fun interactive device—it must be meaningful. Remember that *their* purpose is to help you make *your* key point more memorable.

83 THE LISTENING OPEN

The listening open is perfect for gatherings in which your core purpose is to elicit feedback from the audience. There are two main formats for this type of presentation:

1. **Unrestricted Feedback:** If your goal is to avoid prejudicing the type of feedback the audience provides, you can begin by articulating your intent for the meeting and asking a neutral question to kick off the discussion. "What can management do to help you do your jobs more efficiently?" will provoke different feedback than the more restrictive "Keeping our budget constraints in mind, what can management do to help you do your jobs more efficiently?"

2. **Defined Feedback:** For some presentations, it may be more productive to use the open to create boundaries and define the type of feedback you'd like to receive. One client was concerned that the meeting she was about to lead would devolve into a "gripe" session. To prevent that from happening, she opened by telling her employees that since the problems in their department were already well defined, she wanted to spend their time together discussing possible solutions.

For both options, your intent is less to advocate for a specific point of view than it is to gain a better understanding of theirs. Think of yourself more as a facilitator than as a presenter.

Since audiences are often "cold" at the beginning, warm them up by exhibiting openness. If no one volunteers to speak first, wait a few seconds (someone often feels compelled to break the silence) or call on someone to answer your first question. Be careful not to negatively judge the responses you receive. Instead, acknowledge the feedback and repeat it back to the speaker with neutral language to make sure you understood it.

84 THE ACTIVITY OPEN

Beginning a presentation with an activity can work well for training workshops in which you're teaching a specific skill.

Beyond getting the audience engaged immediately, beginning with an activity can also increase buy-in, particularly if audience members struggle with parts of the activity. (If they do, they will quickly recognize the need for your workshop.) Make sure the activity isn't too simple or it could backfire—if they succeed with ease, your workshop no longer holds a useful purpose.

In their book *Telling Ain't Training*, Harold D. Stolovitch and Erica J. Keeps offer smart advice to trainers:

> "Important to successful learning activities is that they be inherently interesting, even fun. This means that the trainer or training designer should build in elements of challenge, curiosity, and fantasy. For challenge, the activities present difficulties that, with effort, can be overcome to achieve hard-won success. Curiosity means not telling the learners everything at once. The activities have the learners wondering what will happen next. They're curious but not confused."

An audience of high school guidance counselors might be divided into groups of two and presented with a difficult scenario in which a student is threatening to harm himself but begging the counselor to maintain his confidentiality. The American School Counselor Association states that there are "limits to confidentiality when the student poses a threat to self or others." How would you gain that student's trust and counsel him if you can't make a promise of confidentiality? What would you say? After giving each person 10 minutes to conduct that role play, the facilitator would ask where they struggled and then move on to the body of the training, designed to strengthen those weaker areas.

85 THE AUDIENCE COMPETITION OPEN

In training or workshop settings, a brief audience competition can be a terrific way to get your learners actively engaged from the opening moments and set an upbeat and interactive tone for the entire session.

For small groups (10 people or less), you can divide the audience into two teams. For larger groups, you can split the audience into several smaller teams.

In our media training workshops, we sometimes begin by separating a group of eight trainees into two groups of four. We'll provide them with a crisis scenario—perhaps their medical testing facility was damaged by fire last night, which destroyed an undetermined number of time-sensitive patient blood tests—and ask them to appoint a spokesperson and prepare that person for a press conference.

To keep the energy high and the adrenaline pumping, we set a time limit on the exercise. After a set amount of time—say, 10 minutes—we have the spokesperson from each team come to the front of the room and deliver a joint press conference. The team whose spokesperson scores the most "points" wins.

That exercise works because it gives the audience an immediate feel for the time pressures that surround most real-life crises. The exercise is directly related to the workshop's focus.

Similar "competition" exercises can be used in a variety of settings. A grocery store manager can begin a meeting by asking two volunteers to see who can bag groceries the quickest. A music instructor about to discuss breath control can begin by having students compete to see who can hold the longest note. A physician can split an audience of medical residents into groups of three, provide them with a list of mysterious ailments, and see which team can diagnose the ailment correctly first.

86 THE HUMOROUS OPEN

Many speakers are under the mistaken impression that they're supposed to open a presentation with a joke. For most speakers, that's a lousy idea. It seems to be a truism that while everyone *thinks* they're funny, only a few people actually are.

Don't think in terms of "jokes." Think humor—an anecdote, an irresistible irony, a specific reference that only people in that audience would appreciate. And, like every other type of open, make sure the humor ties directly to your message.

Here's an example of a (hopefully humorous) true anecdote about communication disconnects I once used to open a speech:

> "My mother once called her insurance agent and told her she wanted to insure art.
>
> The agent asked, 'Why?' My mother replied, 'Well, in case something happens.'
>
> The agent replied, 'But what do you think is going to happen?' My mother, flustered that her insurance agent didn't seem to understand the purpose of insurance, stammered, 'I don't know. Maybe get stolen? Or damaged?'
>
> 'But why would anyone want to steal art?' the agent snapped.
>
> It was then, at that moment, that my mother realized what was going wrong. [*pause*]
>
> My father's name is Art. [*pause*]
>
> Those types of crossed signals happen in business communication all the time. And they are costing your company time, money, and reputation."

87 | THE SELF-EFFACING OPEN

Self-effacing humor is often considered one of the "safest" forms of humor, since the target of the joke is the speaker him- or herself. In his classic public speaking book *The Quick and Easy Way to Effective Speaking*, Dale Carnegie writes:

> "One of the best ways for a speaker to endear himself to an audience is to play himself down...Audiences open their hearts, as well as their minds, to speakers who deliberately deflate themselves by calling attention to some deficiency or failing on their part, in a humorous sense."

The humor should be only gently self-effacing; stay away from quips that question your credibility on the speech topic itself.

For example, our firm's vice president *could* begin her presentations this way:

> "I am a former journalist with NBC News, during which time I earned an Emmy Award for our election coverage. I produced pieces for *NBC Nightly News* and *The Today Show*, among other programs, and remain friendly today with many high-profile reporters."

That opening—while true and potentially helpful in establishing her credibility with an audience—doesn't come across with humility.

Instead, she simply begins with this:

> "My name is Christina, and I am a recovering journalist."

People usually laugh at that line. And to keep her quip relevant to the topic, Christina quickly transitions to an explanation of how her experience will help members of the audience improve their communication skills during the workshop.

88 THE BORROWED HUMOR OPEN

Some people who aren't particularly funny can be *perceived* as funny simply by borrowing someone else's humor. A strange thing can happen when you quote someone else's humorous line, show a witty cartoon, or pass along a funny story you once heard—the audience gives *you* the credit for being funny. That makes sense; even if you're not the person who originally thought of the humor, you get credit for noticing it and passing it along. And, the audience will figure, only a person who has at least some humor is capable of doing *that*.

When you share something humorous, don't act like you're about to deliver a joke. As James C. Humes once noted, "The difference between a joke and humor is the difference between a pornographic picture and a love scene in a good movie." Your goal is to use humor to reinforce a key takeaway point, not be a professional comic.

Therefore, minimize the setup. Don't announce that you're about to share a "hilarious story." If your story doesn't elicit a laugh, your oversold setup will make it clear to the audience that you bombed—and you will have exposed yourself as a person who's not particularly funny.

Instead, just share whatever piece of humor you intend to offer in the same manner you deliver the rest of your talk. If your material gets a laugh, you can act pleasantly surprised. If it doesn't, nothing is lost—you delivered it in such a way that it can work as a straight line or a humorous one.

I've seen some of the driest presenters score huge humor points, sometimes without even uttering a word. When they finish a point, they click to a slide featuring a funny quote or cartoon. When the audience roars, the speaker gets the credit, regardless of the original source. (You should obviously respect copyrights and give attribution as appropriate.)

89 THE VIDEO CLIP OPEN

Many presentation experts oppose the idea of opening a speech with a video clip. Their argument usually contains two parts:

1. Videos focus the audience's initial attention onto a screen, not you, which means you're subordinate to your technology from the start.

2. Very few people are gifted enough as speakers to effectively compete against a well-produced video, resulting in an inevitable audience letdown when the video ends and you begin.

Both of those arguments are worthy of your consideration. And I share their opposition to showing video clips just because you *can*. But there's a place for video at the beginning of presentations *if* it's used judiciously and strategically.

For example, you might use a video clip when few words could match its power: a product demonstration that can't be done "live" in the room (perhaps a car shown from a driver's perspective going around a racetrack at record speed), shots from a refugee camp housing hundreds of thousands of people, or a news clip highlighting the "characters" or event you'll be discussing during your talk. In each of those cases, it's usually best to begin by setting up the clip before showing it.

Video clips can also be helpful in establishing a mood in the room, but I'd advise against using them as your go-to simply to "pump up the energy." They're more effectively used to *alter* the baseline mood of the audience if it's different from the mood you want to create. In those cases, video can be used to uplift an audience or shift them into a more contemplative mood—just make sure to match the energy of the clip when *it* ends and *you* begin. And do keep your clips short; a minute or two is usually enough. Any more than that, and you're just showing a film.

90 THE AUDIO CLIP OPEN

In his autobiography *An American Life*, Ronald Reagan described the feelings many people in his generation shared about radio:

> "Radio was magic. It was theater of the mind. It forced you to use your imagination. You'd sit in your living room and be transported to glamorous locales around the world."

Television, many people later complained, eliminated the need for audience members to engage more actively by envisioning the events being described for themselves. That, they'd say, stripped imagination from the equation.

The difference between radio and television is similar in impact to the difference between playing an audio clip or a video clip for your audience. That's not to say that one is bad and the other is good, but rather that both play different roles and can have considerably different effects.

The United States Holocaust Memorial Museum in Washington, DC has a room in which you can listen to the oral histories of survivors. Their stories are haunting—and the power of the audio testimonies, at least for me, is that you're able to focus on the words themselves without getting distracted by physical features ("She looks great for her age!" or "He looks lousy.").

Audio clips don't have to be that dramatic to work for your presentations. You can play a voicemail from an angry customer, a quirky radio news report about your new product, or sounds of birds chirping from the tropical rainforest you're about to speak of.

As with video clips, keep the excerpts short. Your purpose is to give your audience a taste, not let the clips overtake your role.

91 THE POWERPOINT OPEN

Little tells an audience that the talk they're about to see is going to be boring more than seeing the speaker begin by clicking to a cluttered slide. PowerPoint (and other similar programs) is overused and, when it is used, tends to be used badly.

The recommended PowerPoint open dispenses with the hackneyed and sleep-inducing agenda slide and begins with a powerful visual that creates curiosity instead.

For example, a presentation about inefficient design might begin with a sharp full-screen image of a home coffee machine.

> "This is a coffeemaker. Like many of the newer coffeemakers, it has an interesting feature. As soon as it finishes brewing a pot of coffee, it lets out a beeping noise to let the owner know the coffee is ready. This is intended to be helpful.
>
> But think about that for a moment. Many people share small apartments or homes, and it's not unusual for one person to wake up before roommates, a partner, or children do. Moments after that bleary-eyed person puts up their morning pot of coffee, that loud 'BEEP! BEEP!' might very well rouse the entire household. And no, these coffeemakers don't have a mute option.
>
> How did such a poorly designed product make it to market? What type of real-life testing should we manufacturers do to avoid such mistakes? And how can we avoid designing features intended to help ('*Your coffee is ready!*') but that actually make life more difficult?"

Used in such a manner, the image of the coffeemaker becomes a powerful symbol of design ineptitude. The slide supports your point *without* becoming a distraction for the audience.

92 THE POLL OPEN

A few other opens in this book are types of "poll" opens, but this lesson focuses on specific technology that allows audiences to take an electronic poll. Some programs allow you to set up a poll using an app and, as your audience votes on a keypad or electronic device, their answers appear in real time on the screen.

Many of our clients are attracted to this type of technology (for understandable reasons), but I always remind them that their use of it has to meet a specific goal, not be used solely to show off technical savvy.

As an example, the Intelligence Squared debate series uses these devices to ask a live audience to vote "for," "against," or "undecided" about a provocative proposition. Just before the debate begins, audience members vote on statements such as "The Constitutional Right to Bear Arms Has Outlived Its Usefulness" or "Affirmative Action on Campus Does More Harm Than Good."

In the middle of the debate, the moderator reveals those vote totals to give the debaters (and the audience) a sense of where audience sentiment stood at the beginning. At the end, the audience votes a second time, and the side that was able to shift the most votes from beginning to end wins.

That is a terrific use of this technology because it is meaningfully tied to the proceedings.

You can use a digital vote at the beginning of your talk to get a baseline understanding of how your audience feels about an issue (be prepared to speak to any possible result), assess the group's familiarity with your topic, or expose a knowledge gap. This option also allows for anonymous voting, which could result in more candid feedback than a group discussion that requires audience members to go "on the record" in public.

93 THE ONLINE TOUR OPEN

Murphy's Law holds that whatever can go wrong, will go wrong—and in my experience that's rarely truer than when someone attempts to conduct a live online demo during a presentation.

Commonly, you'll see these demos when people are releasing a new piece of software or debuting an updated website. The speaker begins by clicking to a page, explaining what's new, and then clicking to another page.

The problem? Internet connections are notoriously unreliable at conference centers and hotels—and placing the success of your entire presentation on an unreliable Wi-Fi signal can be, at best, a high-wire act. Instead of relying on an active Internet connection, a better solution is to record your series of clicks using a program that captures the movement on your computer screen in advance (type "how to record what you're looking at on your computer" into a search engine to find a plethora of options).

Using that option means that you'll have to practice the timing of your narration in advance. Also, you'll have to be prepared to pause the video if an audience member asks a question or something unexpected occurs that throws off your timing.

My general preference is *not* to begin a presentation with an online tour and to set up the demo by offering some meaningful context first. But there are exceptions. For example, if a speaker wants to drive home just how difficult it can be for the average person to locate a customer-service phone number on her company's current website, beginning with a video that shows seven logical but ill-fated clicks could make that point quite effectively.

If you do decide to take the risk and go "live," at least record the clicks in advance as a backup in case the technology fails.

94 THE STUDY HALL OPEN

Let's say you're leading a business meeting and need to share several data-heavy charts and graphs with your audience in order for them to be able to understand and discuss your final recommendations.

You know that projecting the charts via PowerPoint would be ineffective—it's just too much data, and people would likely prefer to flip pages back and forth and make notations.

You also know that if you send the report to people in advance, some of the participants might not read it prior to your meeting. Worse, they could form a different conclusion than the one you had hoped they would—and that opinion could solidify between the time they review your material and the time you meet.

In such situations, Edward Tufte, a well-regarded expert in visual display and a professor emeritus at Yale University, proposes using a "study hall."

He suggests that you begin the session by handing a printout to each attendee and asking them to read the document (which shouldn't be terribly long). Only after you've given everyone sufficient time to review it would you begin your presentation—not by repeating what they've just read, but by adding context and meaning to the data.

Tufte believes this format will, in the not-to-distant future, also take place electronically, with audience members using a more interactive medium, such as an iPad, to review the material.

This format has more of a place during an occasional internal business meeting than a persuasive speech; more during a data-heavy scientific or financial briefing than a presentation to potential clients. I'd also stay away from this format if you're trying to lead an audience to a powerful "aha!" moment.

95 THE "START WITH THE CHORUS" OPEN

Most pop songs begin with a verse and build to a chorus. That formula is so common that the band Genesis released an album in 1981 titled *ABACAB*. They used those letters to represent different parts of their songs: "A" represented the verse, "B" represented the chorus, and "C" represented the bridge. Listen to pop songs on the radio today, and you'll discover that almost all of them still conform to a similar construct.

But a few songs, such as The Beatles' 1963 release "She Loves You," were different. They flipped the script and started with the chorus, or "B," the hook that grabbed the audience's attention from the first note.

This speech starter borrows from such memorable tunes by beginning with your conclusion and working backward to explain how you arrived at it. Such an approach is familiar to anyone who ever watched a legal drama:

> "By the end of this trial, I intend to prove that the defendant is guilty of murder."

That opening salvo is the chorus. The evidence the prosecutor introduces during the trial is the verse.

Here's another example of beginning with the chorus from a more typical workplace setting:

> "We recommend Mega Corporation as our main supplier. After a careful analysis of three companies for this role, it wasn't even close. Today, we'll explain why Mega is the right call for us."

That may not seem terribly unusual, but that same presentation is typically delivered in reverse order: a careful comparison of the three companies first, and the recommendation given last.

96 THE VISUAL OPEN

When people think of the visuals they'd like to use during their presentations, they tend to think in terms of PowerPoint slides. That's unfortunate, because there are *many* other ways to use visuals during the opening of a presentation.

You can use a photograph, a chart printed on poster board, or a physical object such as a scientific specimen or product sample.

A speaker delivering a major keynote speech on advances in technology might begin by asking the hotel staff to wheel a refrigerator onto the stage. (That would obviously need to be prearranged.) The speaker could begin like this:

> "According to pingdom.com, 'The first hard drive to have more than 1 gigabyte in capacity was the IBM 3360 in 1980. It was the size of that refrigerator, weighed 550 pounds, and the price ranged from $81,000 to $142,400.' That machine could store roughly 2.5 gigabytes. You may not know what a gigabyte is, so let me put that into perspective. Today, you can store the same amount of data on *this* [*holds up a USB memory stick barely larger than an adult human thumb*]. And it would cost you about $4."

Less elaborately, lawmakers opposed to a piece of legislation might attack its complexity by dropping the bill—often thousands of pages long—onto a table with a loud "thud." Such theater makes their complaint more memorable.

One client, a scientist, delivered a talk about the Dark Ages. He explained that the darkness was absolute, beyond any darkness that humans living today have ever experienced. In order to drive his point home, he killed the room lights during his description, creating an environment more similar to the one he was describing (and making his the ultimate *nonvisual* visual).

97 THE LIVE DEMO OPEN

Product demonstrations, or "demos," tend to occur in the middle of a presentation, not during the open. The open is typically used to set up the demo by discussing the product, how it was developed, the problem it was intended to solve, and/or its benefits.

But there are times when the product itself is so powerful, so self-explanatory, that simply showing it in action is the most effective open possible.

A blender made by the company Blendtec offers the perfect example. In a series of amusing videos, the brand's founder places improbable products into his blender—an iPhone, golf balls, a soda can—and asks the question: "Will it blend?" As the blades start whirring, the viewer instantly sees the power of the machine. The spokesperson doesn't have to say much at all. The product does the talking.

Proving the power of their demos, Blendtec's videos have been viewed on YouTube more than 260 million times as of May 2015, according to Wikipedia. These savvy commercials even landed the company's founder an appearance on *The Tonight Show*.

This open can also be used if your product is conducive to samples.

As an example, one client, a spirits brand, begins presentations by having a mixologist (a skilled bartender) make a newly concocted cocktail and pass it out to the audience. The product sample itself—which is almost always received enthusiastically—becomes the open. The body of the presentation moves on to discuss how the product is manufactured, why it's unique in the marketplace, and how it can be used to make three other popular adult beverages.

98 THE VOICEOVER OPEN

Imagine you're in a presentation hall when, all of a sudden, the lights dim, a photo appears on the screen, and a speaker—from some unseen location—begins to speak. That "voiceover" option is dramatic and often effective—but because it's so different, it *must* be deployed in a meaningful way.

I've used this when trying to get my audience to develop a deeper understanding of who *their* target audiences are during their speeches. For one group, I displayed a slide of a woman and, from the back of the room where the audience couldn't see me, said:

> "I'd like you to direct your attention to the screen and look at this woman, Kate, as I tell you about her.
>
> Kate is based in Nashville. This is the first time she's attending your conference. She's 46 years old, has two kids, and is one of three employees in her firm. Like most professionals, she has too much to do, and is looking for ways to be more efficient, make more money, and be of more value to her clients.
>
> Your speech, which Kate plans to attend, is scheduled for 11:00 a.m. tomorrow, the third day of the conference. Kate is going out with a few new friends tonight, and won't return to her hotel room until 12:30 a.m. When she wakes up at 6:15 a.m., she's going to be tired and a little hung over. She's also overwhelmed. In the previous two days, she's heard a lot of great ideas, but is struggling with which ones she can implement given her limited time and resources. Given that this is what Kate is going through, it's no easy task for you to get her attention and keep it throughout your presentation. Now multiply Kate by 50 people. *That's* who's in your room."

99 THE "SHOUT IT OUT" OPEN

One client hired our firm to deliver an interactive media training workshop for 30 of her colleagues. During our planning call, she made clear to me that her coworkers were full of energy and good humor, and that they would appreciate being engaged from the very beginning of the session.

I racked my brain to come up with a new, creative idea that would take advantage of their enthusiasm.

The first point I had planned to make dealt with the competition that companies like theirs faced when trying to gain the public's attention. I intended to tell them that since people are barraged with thousands of marketing messages per day—through advertisements, billboards, sales fliers, links on Twitter and Facebook, product placements in movies and television shows, and more—they would have to cut through the clutter more effectively in order to earn the attention they craved.

Finally, I got an idea that would require the audience's help. On the training day, I opened like this:

> "If you look around this room, you'll notice that brand logos and marketing messages are everywhere—on water bottles, your laptops, even on your clothing. For the next 30 seconds, I'd like you to look around the room—and when you see a logo or marketing message, I want you to shout out the brand name as loudly as you possibly can. The clock begins…NOW!"

A cacophony of voices, crashing over one another, responded with great verve for the next half minute: "Apple!" "Microsoft!" "Diet Coke!" "Starbucks!" We shared a good laugh at their boisterous response—but more important, the opening exercise led the audience directly to my first takeaway point and set an upbeat tone for the rest of the workshop.

100 THE DRAMATIC EFFECT OPEN

In the Academy Award-winning documentary *An Inconvenient Truth*, former Vice President Al Gore uses a dramatic technique to demonstrate the atmospheric increase in carbon dioxide (CO_2).

On a screen, he shows where CO_2 is today, which is significantly higher than the historical norm. Then, he discusses where the trend line is headed within 50 years. But before projecting that line onto the screen, he mounts an electric forklift, presses the "up" button, and goes two stories high into the air as the line on the screen goes up in sync with him.

It's a "dramatic" device in that it's not a technique many audiences have seen before. But it worked beautifully because it was memorable—and its power was owed to being tied directly to his message.

One speaker I saw was charged with teaching a molecule chain to a group of culinary students (in the context of food science). The students, who were more interested in cooking than the science behind it, were immediately snapped to attention when the speaker stood up on a stool and drew a 6-foot long molecular chain on the wall behind him (the wall was made of erasable white tile). Not only did that speaker use the chain throughout his entire talk, but his technique signaled to his students that they were about to learn something more interesting than they had expected.

Over the years, I've seen a lot of "dramatic effect" opens, including a speaker who began a talk by singing a song, another who wore an elaborate costume, and another who ran in from the back of the room, bounded up the stage stairs, and leapt atop a chair. In all of those cases, my guidance was the same: a dramatic open, which by its very nature calls attention to itself, must be used (if at all) by experienced speakers for only one purpose, which is to make your message more memorable.

101 THE BAD OPEN

I've reserved this final lesson to discuss the things speakers often do to begin their presentations—but shouldn't.

First, don't begin by telling the audience how nervous you are or by issuing an apology for your imperfect speaking skills. One of the great benefits of preparing an engaging open is that your audiences will be interested in hearing you from the start, eliminating the need for such disclaimers.

Second, don't begin by saying things such as "I know it's early and you're probably tired" or "I know it was a late night for many of you last night, so I'll try to keep things lively." In those cases, it's best to transport the audience to a more awake state by engaging them early with great content. Putting a fine point on their fatigue is not only cliché, but also calls more attention to it.

Finally, my single biggest pet peeve is when people admit that they're unprepared. One speaker I observed began with this:

> "I was asked to speak for 20 minutes. I have a lot of notes here, so we'll see how far I get."

That obvious lack of preparation sent an immediate signal that the speaker didn't think the audience was important enough to warrant a well-organized presentation that honored its time.

I'll close this section with a final thought: nothing about your presentation, including your open, has to be "perfect." In fact, "perfect" speakers often come across as overly rehearsed and inauthentic. Simply by respecting your audience's time with a thoughtfully constructed presentation and delivering your talk with the passion and energy it deserves, you can accomplish almost every goal you had set out to achieve. I hope the ideas in this book help you in that effort for many years to come.

Selecting The Right Open

"You had me at 'hello.'"

Dorothy Boyd (Renée Zellweger) to Jerry Maguire (Tom Cruise)
in the film Jerry Maguire

Selecting The Right Open

Now that you've been exposed to 101 different options for opening a presentation, you might be wondering how to decide which of them to use for yours. After all, for any given topic, you could probably use 10, 25, maybe even 50 of the opens in this book—and many of them would work quite well.

For that reason, there's no single rule to follow when selecting an open. Some opens are obviously better for some occasions than others—you wouldn't use a "live demo" open without a product to show off—but many others can be used for virtually any occasion.

For example, you might think scientists would be most receptive to a logical, data-based argument. But sometimes, a well-chosen anecdote highlighting an understandable but preventable flaw in a fellow scientist's work can prove more persuasive.

To help narrow your choices, think carefully about the audience, your goals for the presentation, and the mood you're hoping to create in the room.

You would probably use a different open for enthusiastic volunteers than for skeptical employees, or for knowledgeable professionals rather than college freshmen. But even there, the same *type* of open can work for both audiences, even if the specific information you convey during each would be different.

Your goal for the talk can also help determine the best open. Speeches intended to inform, motivate, persuade, or elicit input each benefit from different approaches. If your intent is to teach students a skill, you might introduce a mnemonic device or metaphor that serves as a "mental shortcut." If your aim is to get people involved in a cause, a rhetorical question that gets people thinking or an autobiographical open that shares how you got involved might work best. If you want the audience to understand why your topic matters but anticipate some resistance, an open emphasizing its relevance or that quotes an incorrect but widely held misperception about it might help attract their interest.

The open you choose will also determine the tone you create in the room. Be mindful of whether the open is more likely to create a contemplative, excited, or hopeful mood in the room—any of which can be appropriate.

Above all, I encourage you to experiment. Before your next presentation, challenge yourself to create five different types of opens, and test them by standing up and delivering each out loud. You might find that a couple of them fit you, your topic, and the audience well, while the others don't. Trust that instinct.

But be careful not to gravitate only toward the opens you're already the most comfortable with. Stretch yourself. Try using opens you ordinarily wouldn't. You may still lean on certain types of speech starters more often than others, but it's always a good idea to add a few new colors to your rhetorical palette.

If you're overwhelmed by the number of options, just pick one. It's more important to seek gradual improvement than to allow a quest for perfection—if such a thing exists—to get in your way.

Finally, note how *other* speakers begin their presentations. Write down the ones that worked well and analyze why they succeeded. When speakers begin badly, ask yourself how those presenters could have made their information more compelling. You will *never* attend a boring speech again—*if* you use your time in the audience to analyze what's working, what's not, and how the topic could be presented more effectively.

Whichever open you choose, the fact that you've read this far means that you're going to be dramatically more thoughtful about selecting a compelling grabber than the majority of speakers. Thank you for reading, and as they say on the stage, "Break a leg!"

Acknowledgments

Many of the opens in this book were the result of work we've done with our clients. Some of them wouldn't have emerged without our discussions and their ideas, and a few of them were more the result of their creativity than mine.

Many other authors are cited in this book. Their inspiration and smart thinking have made me a better presentation coach, and I hope you'll consider supporting their work.

Amtrak, on which I wrote many of these pages during business trips, deserves recognition. Its quiet cars make work possible, and the conductors who enforced the 'quiet' rules have my particular gratitude.

Taegan Goddard of Political Wire pushed me to write this book years before I had planned to. You might not be reading it now if it hadn't have been for his gentle prodding.

Andrew Rosenberg, who edited this book and *The Media Training Bible*, is a true professional. Any typos in this book are mine; the ones you don't see are due to his sharp eye.

Friend and trademark attorney Erik Pelton ensures that the excerpts used in this book respect their copyright owners.

My cousin Joanne Levine set me on the path to working in a newsroom. Had she not, I never would have become a media and presentation trainer. My thanks to her are overdue by a couple of decades, but I hope she'll accept them anyway.

Finally, to my wife, who took on additional parenting duties while I completed this book. She would have been justified in asking me to shelve this project for a while. Instead, she encouraged it. Thanks, babe.

Sources

Introduction, Take Two: Winerman, Lea. "'Thin Slices' of Life." American Psychological Association. March 1, 2005.

Introduction, Take Two: Gladwell, Malcolm. *Blink: The Power of Thinking Without Thinking.* New York: Back Bay Books, 2007.

Introduction, Take Two: Medina, John. *Brain Rules: 12 Principles for Surviving and Thriving at Work, Home, and School.* Seattle: Pear Press, 2008.

About This Book: Bligh, Donald A. *What's The Use of Lectures?* San Francisco: Jossey-Bass, 2000.

The Pre-Open, Opens 9 & 88: Humes, James C. *Speak Like Churchill, Stand Like Lincoln: 21 Powerful Secrets of History's Greatest Speakers.* New York: Three Rivers Press, 2002.

The Pre-Open: Perlman, Alan M. *Writing Great Speeches: Professional Techniques You Can Use.* Needham Heights: Allyn and Bacon, 1998.

The Post-Open: Dean, Fletcher. *10 Steps to Writing a Vital Speech.* Phoenix: McMurry Inc., 2011.

The Post-Open & Open 84: Stolovitch, Harold D. and Erica J. Keeps. *Telling Ain't Training, Second Edition.* Alexandria: ASTD Press, 2011.

Open 1: Weinschenk, Susan M. *100 Things Every Presenter Needs To Know About People.* Berkeley: New Riders, 2012.

Open 3: Kepner, Charles H. and Benjamin B. Tregoe. *The New Rational Manager: An Updated Edition for the New World.* Princeton: Princeton Research Press, 2013.

Opens 3 & 71: Duarte, Nancy. *Resonate: Present Visual Stories That Transform Audiences.* Hoboken: John Wiley & Sons, Inc., 2010.

Open 13: Crystal, Billy. *Still Foolin' 'Em: Where I've Been, Where I'm Going, and Where the Hell Are My Keys?* New York: Henry Holt & Co., 2013.

Open 14: Lewinsky, Monica. The Price of Shame. March 2015. Retrieved from http://www.ted.com/talks/monica_lewinsky_the_price_of_shame?language=en

Open 15: Negron, Taylor. California Gothic. December 16, 2014. Retrieved from http://themoth.org/posts/storytellers/taylor-negron

Opens 15 & 27: Heath, Chip, and Dan Heath. *Made to Stick: Why Some Ideas Survive and Others Die.* New York: Hyperion, 2006.

Open 17: Feeney, Rob. Testimony to Chattanooga, Tennessee City Council. Spring 2011. Retrieved from https://www.youtube.com/watch?v=Pp9-CI68cXU.

Open 19: Lehane, Christopher, Mark Fabiani, and Bill Guttentag. *Masters of Disaster: The Ten Commandments of Damage Control.* New York: Palgrave Macmillan, 2012.

Open 20: Carlson, Adam. "Former Football Players' Suicides Tied to Concussions." Atlanta Journal-Constitution. December 1, 2014.

Open 22: Simmons, Annette. *The Story Factor: Inspiration, Influence, and Persuasion Through the Art of Storytelling.* Cambridge: Basic Books, 2006.

Opens 24 & 69: Abela, Andrew. *Advanced Presentations by Design: Creating Communication That Drives Action, Second Edition.* San Francisco: Pfeiffer, 2013.

Open 25: Reynolds, Garr. *Presentation Zen: Simple Ideas on Presentation Design and Delivery, Second Edition.* Berkeley: New Riders, 2012.

Open 26: Simon, Paul. At The Zoo [Recorded by Simon & Garfunkel]. On *Bookends.* New York City: Columbia. (January 8, 1967)

Open 26: Howard, Maria. "Allegory in Literature: History, Definition & Examples." Study.com.

Open 28: Frost, Robert. "The Road Not Taken." The Norton Anthology of Modern Poetry. Eds. Richard Ellman and Robert O'Clair. New York: W.W. Norton & Company, 1973.

Open 29: Shute, Nancy. "Exercise Info, Not Calorie Counts, Helps Teens Drop Sodas." NPR. December 16, 2011.

Open 30: Sandberg, Sheryl. Why We Have Too Few Women Leaders. December 2010. Retrieved from http://www.ted.com/talks/sheryl_sandberg_why_we_have_too_few_women_leaders?language=en

Open 32: Merchant, Nilofer. Got a Meeting? Take a Walk. February 2013. Retrieved from http://www.ted.com/talks/nilofer_merchant_got_a_meeting_take_a_walk?language=en

Open 32: Meyer, Pamela. How to Spot a Liar. July 2011. Retrieved from http://www.ted.com/talks/pamela_meyer_how_to_spot_a_liar?language=en

Open 33: Sinek, Simon. Keynote Speech, CHC Safety Summit Gala Dinner. May 2013. Retrieved from https://www.youtube.com/watch?v=NHxxhu5ldw8

Open 35: Phillips, Tom. "42 Incredibly Weird Facts You'll Want to Tell All Your Friends." BuzzFeed. March 26, 2014.

Open 37: Holderness, Cates. "What Colors Are This Dress?" BuzzFeed. February 26, 2015.

Open 38: Kasper, Justin. Uncharted Territory: From Deep Oceans to Deep Space. July 2013. Retrieved from https://www.youtube.com/watch?v=IboAA76XwXM

Open 44: "Radio In The 1930's." Radio Stratosphere. Accessed May 7, 2015.

Open 45: Dietz, Karen, and Lori L. Silverman. Business Storytelling for Dummies. Hoboken: John Wiley & Sons, 2013.

Open 47: Jardine, Alexandra. "New York-Presbyterian Delivers Big Message with Quiet Campaign." Advertising Age. May 23, 2012.

Opens 47 & 69: Cialdini, Robert B. *Influence: Science and Practice, Fifth Edition.* Boston: Pearson Education, Inc., 2009.

Open 51: Ballaro, Beverly. "Six Ways To Grab Your Audience Right From The Start." In Presentations That Persuade and Motivate. Boston: Harvard Business School Press, 2004.

Open 51: Solomon, Andrew. Depression, The Secret We Share. October 2013. Retrieved from http://www.ted.com/talks/andrew_solomon_depression_the_secret_we_share?language=en

Open 54: Gallo, David. Underwater Astonishments. March 2007. Retrieved from http://www.ted.com/talks/david_gallo_shows_underwater_astonishments?language=en

Open 54: Rosenbaum, Thane. Matthew Weiner In Conversation with Thane Rosenbaum. New York City: Forum on Law, Culture & Society at the 92nd Street Y, December 2010.

Open 58: Stromberg, Joseph. "Top Ten Mysteries of the Universe." Smithsonian. May 7, 2012.

Opens 59 & 76: Loewenstein, George. "The Psychology of Curiosity: A Review and Reinterpretation." Psychological Bulletin 116, no. 1 (1994): 75-98.

Open 61; Pausch, Randy. Last Lecture: Achieving Your Childhood Dreams. September 2007. Retrieved from https://www.youtube.com/watch?v=ji5_MqicxSo

Open 61: "How To Structure a Persuasive Speech." In Presentations That Persuade and Motivate. Boston: Harvard Business School Press, 2004.

Open 64: Schramm, JD. Break The Silence For Suicide Attempt Survivors. March 2011. Retrieved from http://www.ted.com/talks/jd_schramm?language=en

Open 66: "The Decision to Go to the Moon: President John F. Kennedy's May 25, 1961 Speech Before Congress." NASA History Office.

Open 67: Pacino, Al. *Any Given Sunday.* Film. Directed by Oliver Stone. Burbank: Warner Bros., 1999.

Open 68: Heath, Chip and Dan Heath. *Switch: How To Change Things When Change Is Hard.* New York: Broadway Books, 2010.

Open 75: Luntz, Frank I. *Words That Work: It's Not What You Say, It's What People Hear.* New York: Hyperion, 2006.

Open 75: Roy, Deb. The Birth of a Word. March 2011. Retrieved from http://www.ted.com/talks/deb_roy_the_birth_of_a_word

Open 77: "Brain Teaser: Can You Count?" SharpBrains. September 10, 2006.

Open 77: Jennings, James. "Zillow Confirms That Starbucks Fuels Your Morning, and Gentrification." Philadelphia Magazine. January 29, 2015.

Open 78: "2013 Survey of Americans on the U.S. Role in Global Health." Kaiser Family Foundation. November 7, 2013.

Open 82: Robbins, Apollo. The Art of Misdirection. June 2013. Retrieved from http://www.ted.com/talks/apollo_robbins_the_art_of_misdirection?language=en

Open 87: Carnegie, Dale. *The Quick & Easy Way to Effective Speaking: Modern Techniques For Dynamic Communication.* New York: Pocket Books, 1962.

Open 90: Reagan, Ronald. *An American Life.* New York: Pocket Books, 1990.

Open 94: Tufte, Edward. Presenting Data and Information. New York City: Manhattan Center Studios, October 10, 2013.

Open 96: "Amazing Facts and Figures about the Evolution of Hard Disk Drives." Pingdom Royal. February 8, 2010.

Photo Credits

Euripides and Samuel Johnson photos: Public domain, photographer unknown; Reneé Zellweger photo credit: David Shankbone via Wikimedia. I found the Samuel Johnson and Reneé Zellweger quotes on sparkpresentations.com, and owe a tip of the hat to Andy Saks.

About Brad Phillips

Brad Phillips is the president of Phillips Media Relations, a media and presentation training firm with offices in New York City and Washington, DC.

He is also the author of *The Media Training Bible: 101 Things You Absolutely, Positively Need to Know Before Your Next Interview*, which reached number one on Amazon's PR best sellers list.

Mr. Phillips has trained thousands of media spokespersons and public speakers, including hundreds of top-level executives.

He founded Phillips Media Relations in 2004 after working for several years as a broadcast journalist. After beginning his career as an on-air radio announcer, he worked for *ABC's Nightline with Ted Koppel*. He then moved to CNN, where he helped produce two weekly programs: the media analysis program, *Reliable Sources*, and the political round-table *The Capital Gang*. He was also a contributing producer to *Late Edition with Wolf Blitzer*.

Mr. Phillips is the author of the Mr. Media Training Blog (MrMediaTraining.com), the world's most-visited media training website. The blog regularly covers topics related to public speaking and reviews high-profile speeches. He tweets at @MrMediaTraining.

To learn more about how our firm can help you, please visit PhillipsMediaRelations.com or email us at Info@PhillipsMedia Relations.com.

Quantity Discounts

We offer a quantity discount on the paperback edition of *101 Ways to Open a Speech* for groups interested in purchasing 20 copies or more.

If you would like to inquire about receiving a quantity discount, please email us at books@speakgoodpress.com.

Will You Help This Book?

If you enjoyed this book, I'd be very grateful if you would spread the word.

A five-star review on Amazon is particularly helpful, as potential buyers rely on a book's reviews to help make their purchasing decisions.

You can also order copies for your clients and colleagues. Use the email address above if you'd like a discount on a bulk order.

If you're a teacher or professor, you can help by putting this book on your syllabus. We'd be happy to work with your campus bookstore to arrange a discount.

If you're active on social media, please leave a link for this book along with a comment about how it helped you. If you write a blog, please consider posting a book review.

Finally, you can help this book by letting me know if I missed one of your favorite opens or if you have a great example of an open described in the book. If you do, please email it to books@speakgoodpress.com. I may use your feedback in a future edition of the book or on the Mr. Media Training Blog. Thank you, and good luck!